T0383185

Paradox and Imperatives in Health Care

Redirecting Reform for Efficiency and Effectiveness

Revised Edition

Paradox and Imperatives in Health Care

Redirecting Reform for Efficiency and Effectiveness

Revised Edition

Jeffrey C. Bauer

CRC Press
Taylor & Francis Group
Boca Raton London New York

CRC Press is an imprint of the
Taylor & Francis Group, an **informa** business

A PRODUCTIVITY PRESS BOOK

CRC Press
Taylor & Francis Group
6000 Broken Sound Parkway NW, Suite 300
Boca Raton, FL 33487-2742

© 2015 by Taylor & Francis Group, LLC
CRC Press is an imprint of Taylor & Francis Group, an Informa business

No claim to original U.S. Government works

Printed on acid-free paper
Version Date: 20140618

International Standard Book Number-13: 978-1-4665-9324-4 (Hardback)

Library of Congress Cataloging-in-Publication Data

Bauer, Jeffrey C., author.
    Paradox and imperatives in health care : redirecting reform for efficiency and effectiveness / Jeffrey C. Bauer. -- Revised edition.
        p. ; cm.
    Includes bibliographical references and index.
    Summary: "Most hospitals, health systems, and other provider organizations in the U.S. are still facing financial peril from continuing cuts in Medicare, new federal legislation, and a precarious economic environment. The second edition of this book updates analysis, forecasts, and recommendations made by the author. The book discusses the evolution of the Affordable Care Act, related regulatory trends, and changes in the roles and the business models of third-party health insurers. It also includes an expanded focus on the relative strengths and weaknesses of different business models for organizing the delivery of care, Case studies are included"--Provided by publisher.
        ISBN 978-1-4665-9324-4 (hardcover : alk. paper)
        I. Title.
    [DNLM: 1. Hospital Administration--economics--United States. 2. Efficiency, Organizational--United States. 3. Health Care Reform--United States. 4. Information Management--United States. 5. Organizational Innovation--economics--United States. WX 157 AA1]

    RA971.3
    362.1068--dc23   2014018595

Visit the Taylor & Francis Web site at
http://www.taylorandfrancis.com

and the CRC Press Web site at
http://www.crcpress.com

Dedicated to my sources of inspiration and courage to create

Gustav Mahler
Pierre Boulez
René Magritte
Sol LeWitt

Contents

Chapter 1

Introduction:
The Paradox

> Surely we will end up where we are headed if we do
> not change direction.
>
> **—Confucius**

Back in 2007 when Mark Hagland and I solicited comments on our original concept for a book about performance improvement, several health care executives responded with a question: Why would a provider want to cut costs or improve quality? After all, they argued, the reimbursement system does not provide incentives to reduce costs, and the rewards for quality can be pretty small with respect to the required effort. Reimbursement can even penalize performance improvement initiatives. These experienced leaders indicated no interest in reading a book on efficiency and effectiveness until the federal government required them to take action.

Other executives took the opposite position. They believed our proposed focus was important—so important that they had, in their opinions, already removed all the waste from their organizations. They probably would not read our book because there was nothing more they could do to save money in operations. Nevertheless, they encouraged us to write it because they thought other hospitals needed to get the message. (We expected they also needed it. There is *always* room for improvement.)

We decided to write the book because most executives were in the middle, generally cynical but receptive to new perspectives and responsive solutions. They acknowledged the disincentives that have thwarted past efforts to change a production process or business model. However, they also sensed an unprecedented convergence of forces that compelled action. They wanted a practical guide that would help them survive and, it was hoped, thrive in a potentially hostile environment. All agreed that the status quo was unsustainable in the long run, but none anticipated the two seismic shifts that were just around the corner—the economic collapse of 2008 and the Affordable Care Act (ACA) of 2010.

Dark clouds have always hovered over the medical marketplace, but they had a silver lining in the past. Intense political action could always be counted on to reverse announced cuts in government health programs. Playing hardball with managed care plans would ultimately yield a viable contract, and reimbursement from private insurance could be counted on to compensate for Medicare's lower rates. Better collections procedures could be implemented to manage receivables and cash flow. Keeping revenue above expenses was never easy, but with hard work in the finance department, it could be done.

Key factors in this equation began to change, slowly but relentlessly, with the arrival of the twenty-first century. Government austerity and rapid increases in consumers' financial responsibility started creating an uncommonly gloomy outlook for providers' revenue. High-deductible health plans increasingly became the rule, not the exception. Receivables began rising precipitously, even for patients covered by good commercial insurance. Costs for supplies and labor also started increasing at higher rates. Regulations continued to grow in number and complexity, with serious penalties for noncompliance. Troubling trends in national and international economics cast doubt on any prospects for improvement in public or private capacity to pay for health care. And, "medical tourism" began to draw a perceptible number of patients, with and without insurance, to hospitals in other countries.

The Paradox

The phenomenon of international medical travel points to the paradox of health care in the United States. Americans can often obtain a better deal buying individual medical services in other countries. At home, they spend more on health care than their counterparts anywhere else in the world, both individually and collectively, yet their country is found at or near the bottom of lists that rank the return on investment in medical spending for developed economies. Every other modern country spends significantly less on health care than the United States and generally has a healthier population.

In terms of rational economic theory, the country with the highest per capita expenditures on health care ought to be the country with the healthiest people. But, common sense is contradicted by the facts. The US economy allocates a bit more than 17% of gross domestic product each year to its medical sector, yet its residents do not live as long or as well as those of three dozen comparable countries that devote 12% or less of their economic resources to hospitals, doctors, drugs, and related goods and services. Other developed, postindustrial countries produce at least as much health for their populations with approximately 30% fewer resources (i.e., 17% reduced by 30% is approximately 12%).

Even though its national leaders persistently proclaim the United States has the world's best health care system, economic and epidemiological data show it does not. However, the paradox has an exception that proves the rule and supports the positive focus of this book: The world's best providers of health care are based in the United States, and the rest of the world knows it. Foreigners do not come permanently to the United States just to obtain better health care; they emigrate for other reasons. However, they frequently come to the United States as reverse medical tourists when they need the best health care for a life-threatening condition (admittedly, when cost is not a consideration).

Independent, private health systems based in Rochester (MN), Houston, Boston, Cleveland, New York City, Danville (PA), Oakland (CA), and a few other American cities are internationally recognized for providing the world's best health care—even though they are located in a country that does not. To add irony to paradox, these systems grew out of local initiative and individual vision, and they are extremely different in the way they are organized and managed. They represent the best of American innovation and diversity. Yet, not one of America's world-class medical enterprises was created in response to government imperatives, and they have continued to thrive independent of federal reforms—another key point reflected in this book and its recommendations.

On the one hand, the health care delivery system in the United States is plagued by serious cost, quality, and access problems that are not being solved by law or regulation. On the other hand, some American providers deliver the best care in the world. I believe this paradox can be resolved, but the history of government-driven health reform over the past 50 years and political circumstances for the foreseeable future suggest that another approach is needed. If the United States truly aspires to international exceptionalism in health care, its leaders must take us in a new and different direction to create the world's best health care system—one that produces the top return per dollar spent on population health. This book proposes such a path.

The Imperatives

The economic and political siege on providers and their business partners has accelerated dramatically since the first edition of this book was published in early 2008. However, no guardian angel is approaching to save supply-side organizations from this assault. Public and private purchasers who provided additional money in the past do not have any spare resources to help now or in the foreseeable future. They have reached the limits of their ability and willingness to spend more on health care from one year to the next. And, consumers now have "skin in the game"—thanks to a core concept of the current approach to health reform—but their disposable income has not risen to meet the increasing financial obligations that have suddenly been thrust on them.

The underlying circumstances are not only different now, but also unprecedented. Learning to "game the system" and complaining about the obvious flaws with reimbursement also do not work any more. The latest reform laws offer some additional payment for meeting quality benchmarks and using electronic records according to federal standards, but the dollar value of the incentives is probably less than the cost of making the investment to qualify for them—not to mention the risk of being asked to return the payments for noncompliance with ambiguous and changing regulations. Previously reliable sources of income growth have all but disappeared since 2008. If they have not done so already, providers must start drawing on their own resources and resourcefulness to survive the next two or three years.

The good news for the future of health care in the United States is that providers and their business partners have an internal resource to draw on—the pervasive waste generated by inefficient and ineffective production processes. Resources are abundantly, even shamefully, wasted in the delivery of health care services. The transformative process of redirecting wasted resources to productive use within the medical enterprise is the central focus of this book. Becoming efficient and effective is the only way that the vast majority of providers will be able to stay in business as purchasers, payers, and patients refuse to keep paying more for health care.

Of course, the American reimbursement system is also exceptionally wasteful. The first edition of this book in early 2008 identified many dysfunctional aspects of reimbursement but did not anticipate them being addressed in the foreseeable future. Quite unexpectedly—surprising because the president we elected late in 2008 had taken very different positions on health reform as a candidate—the ACA of 2010 outlawed several insurance practices (e.g., exclusion of coverage for preexisting conditions, lifetime limits on total value of benefits, experience rating) that had created financial problems for patients and providers alike for several decades. Whether the law provides long-term solutions for these problems is uncertain as this second edition goes to press in mid-2014, but implementation is not proceeding smoothly toward its presumed goal.

The law's inept launch and unintended consequences seem to be creating at least one new problem for every old one it sought to solve, supporting the theory that the greatest cause of problems is solutions. Providers betting their futures solely on the ACA's intent to provide more Americans with health insurance will be lucky to survive for long. More than ever, the keys to survival and growth are performance improvement and organizational transformation. The ACA addresses some serious flaws in reimbursement, but it will not diminish payers' intense and justified attacks on providers' high costs and inconsistent quality. The ACA sets the stage for the next act in the ongoing drama of health care and reinforces the imperatives for providers to play their roles efficiently and effectively—or be driven out of business.

Analytical Foundation for Solutions

This book integrates four levels of analysis that collectively explain why and how health care organizations must transform their internal operations to survive in the new marketplace.

■ The first level of analysis identifies new realities that will not be kind to "business as usual" in hospitals, medical groups, and other provider organizations because the future will be significantly different from the past. Providers must develop new responses to new circumstances because strategies that worked in the past are increasingly irrelevant, or even lethal. In particular, the implications of federally mandated health reform are put in perspective so that organizational leaders will recognize the need to focus their efforts on the forces they can control.

■ The second level of analysis delves directly into the waste that exists throughout the health care delivery system. Economic concepts of efficiency and effectiveness are explained and applied in practical terms to expose the remarkable volume of resources that could be redirected to produce less-expensive health care services of acceptable quality. This level of the analysis addresses the opportunity costs of dysfunctional production processes— that is, the better economic and clinical results that could be achieved if wasted resources were redirected to productive use for the benefit of population health.

■ The third analytical level identifies proven processes for efficient and effective production, including appropriate adoption of information and communication technologies. It applies important lessons that can be learned from other industries forced to change, often quite quickly, to stay in business when customers were no longer willing to deal on traditional terms. The discussion also identifies tools that successful health care delivery organizations are using to improve their performance (e.g., Lean, Six Sigma).

■ The fourth level of analysis explores leadership's strategic role in structuring organizational responses to the new imperatives. It shows how trustees and senior executives can initiate and oversee the necessary transformation from fighting external threats to guiding internal changes that reduce costs and improve outcomes—the real business of health care. It also recommends specific strategies for creating the world's best health care delivery system through private innovation that actualizes the best potential of local marketplaces, not government mandates that try to create a "one-size-fits-all" national system.

These levels of analysis are interwoven throughout the book, and the final chapter presents three specific recommendations for local initiatives undertaken by multistakeholder partnerships, accountably and transparently. The book's ultimate goal is to put the health care delivery system on a good path while redirection is still possible.

The Target Audience

This book is written primarily for the leaders of provider organizations and their business partners. The content is specifically presented from a strategic perspective, giving decision makers enough knowledge to recognize transformational changes that must be considered and can be made. Board members, senior executives, and chief clinical officers will find the information they need to set a new course, to hire content experts to help them plan the journey, and to hold these experts accountable for the success of their work. In other words, this book prepares leaders for deciding what needs to be done and selecting tools that can be used to operate efficiently and effectively. It is not an in-depth guide for managing the daily tasks of performance improvement.

Although the target audience is health care's decision makers, this book should be equally useful to purchasers, payers, elected officials, regulators, policy analysts, patients, and other stakeholders committed to building a better medical marketplace. I also hope it will influence the political debate over health reform, turning elected officials and policy makers away from casting blame for the system's past failures to creating consensus for its future success. It can also be used as a resource for improving the strained relations between customers on the demand side and providers on the supply side through multistakeholder partnerships focused on operating efficiently and effectively in pursuit of common goals. Visionary leaders on the demand side of the market should use this book to start thinking about getting their own houses in order. Every stakeholder in health care could be doing better. This book should be helpful to all.

Note on Authorship

The first edition was cowritten with Mark Hagland, an award-winning journalist who has covered the delivery of health care for more than 25 years. Mark's current position as editor in chief of *Healthcare Informatics* prevents him from being involved in this revision. I wish for several reasons that circumstances would have allowed Mark to remain as coauthor. His remarkable skills as an interviewer and researcher are particularly missed, and I simply cannot match his ability to create case studies like those that illustrated key points in the first edition.

Fortunately, Mark compiled another volume of illustrative case studies (*Transformative Quality: The Emerging Revolution in Health Care Performance*; CRC Press, Boca Raton, FL,

2008) after we jointly wrote the first edition of *Paradox and Imperatives*. I strongly recommend Mark's second work to readers who seek even more examples of performance improvement as applied in successful provider organizations. Mark's ongoing articles in *Healthcare Informatics* also provide up-to-date information on successful implementation of performance improvement programs in provider organizations.

As only author of the revised edition, I am solely responsible for all content in these pages. The observations and opinions that follow are based on my 45 years of firsthand experience with just about every aspect of health care delivery. This book clearly reflects my disappointment with the dysfunctional marketplace that has evolved over those years, but it also displays my firm belief that visionary leaders who understand the paradox and imperatives can create exemplary health care systems. I am an insider who cares deeply about American health care—a constructive contrarian disturbed by the present but excited by possibilities for the future. Consequently, this book goes beyond hackneyed discussion of things too often gone wrong to achievable solutions for doing things right all the time, as inexpensively as possible.

Chapter 2

The Economic Challenge: Chaos

cha·os *noun* \'kā-ˌäs\: complete confusion and disorder: a state in which behavior and events are not controlled by anything

(Merriam-Webster Dictionary)

This chapter's title in the first edition (2008) was "The Economic Challenge: Impending Chaos." I have deleted *Impending* in the update because chaos clearly arrived over the intervening years. Even though the Affordable Care Act (ACA) was not foreseeable in 2008, state and federal governments' accumulating failures to implement the law as enacted have created widespread confusion and disorder in the medical marketplace. No identifiable entity is in control of health care's destiny today, and nobody knows for sure where things are headed—sure signs of chaos.

To show how much and how quickly the situation destabilized, the previous Chapter 1 opened just six years ago with a quote widely used in commentaries on health care at the time, Charles Dickens' paradoxical reference to "the best of times and the worst of times." The image resonated with the then-prevalent outlook of health care's leaders. Solid growth had returned to the industry after the 9/11 and dot.com disasters of 2001, but resources were not as abundant as they had been in the previous decade. A few persistent financial problems had been brought under control as leaders focused effort on new business practices like revenue cycle management and automation of patient accounting. And, some serious economic threats had not materialized as predicted, thanks in particular to low interest rates and relatively easy access to capital.

Providers seemed to be generally comfortable with their situations in early 2008. Few were voluntarily undertaking drastic actions to prepare for rough years ahead. Most disagreed with the original first chapter's forecast of impending chaos. However, I was not the only health futurist to foretell earth-shattering change then. Other prominent prognosticators' outlooks included metaphorical references to tsunamis, earthquakes, or the calm before a storm. Regardless of the images appearing in health futurists' crystal balls back then, the profound and unprecedented change we envisioned is here—now and for the foreseeable future. Health care providers are unquestionably facing unprecedented uncertainty: in a word, chaos.

For reasons elaborated throughout this book, leaders in chaotic times can no longer rely on health care's historic abilities to survive external threats by preserving the status quo. Economic and political circumstances in the past had always ensured organizational survival. Purchasers and payers could afford to relent after telling the provider community they were going to put an end to annual increases in medical costs; their own economic growth allowed them to spend a little more on health care, once all was said and done. Governments, private employers, and third-party intermediaries who threatened to stop paying more for health care were taken about as seriously as Chicken Little: The sky never fell as promised, year after year.

End of Growth in Spending: The New Normal

Providers grew accustomed to surviving constant economic threats because health care's portion of the economic "pie" grew every year since the 1960s. Well, those days are over. Current trends and new circumstances suggest that the relative size of the medical economy—the percentage of gross domestic product (GDP) spent on final medical goods and services— has most likely peaked for the foreseeable future. Providers should consequently assume that health care is no longer a growing sector of the economy, and they should change their business models and operations accordingly.

Nobody should be surprised to see health care's growth come to an end. It has been expected for a long time. Indeed, if opponents in every health reform battle of the past several decades had agreed on one thing, it would be that growth in health spending was unsustainable—that there was a limit to what the country could afford to spend on medical goods and services. Nobody ever believed that the medical sector would grow until it consumed every dollar spent by Americans. Man does not live by medical care alone.

Reform advocates of all persuasions have always believed that a limit would be reached, just not right away. Well, for important reasons discussed in this section, the medical economy has finally reached the point at which automatic increases in spending are coming to their unavoidable end. These "new normal" reasons should be taken into account in all subsequent discussions of ways to put American health care on a better path.

Dramatic Decline in Overall Economic Growth

Economic growth has stalled, domestically and globally, for the foreseeable future. Political instability, governmental dysfunction, climate change, inept leadership, financial destabilization, resource depletion, demographic upheaval, widespread terrorism, and other equally disruptive changes have eroded the historic foundations of continued economic growth around the world. New factors of production, especially information and communications technologies, have produced remarkable advances in some areas of economic activity, but not enough to counterbalance the accumulating negative forces. Indeed, zero net economic growth is arguably the optimistic view for the long-term future, given everything that could go wrong in the coming years (e.g., collapse of the pension system, massive defaults on student loans, resurgent bank failures because of overvalued assets and inadequate reserves, and regional economies destroyed by natural disasters). Upside factors are few in comparison.

A big part of the problem is economists' lack of understanding of the twenty-first-century economy, coupled with their proclivity to address its problems with twentieth-century tools. As Alan Greenspan observed in 2006 in his final days as revered chairman of the Federal Reserve System, nobody really knows how the economy works any more. (As proof, he certainly did not foresee the 2008 financial disaster that was brewing on his watch.) His successor, Ben Bernanke, effectively made the same point on leaving office in 2014. The economy is now full of surprises, which means that once-reliable principles for guiding the economy are suddenly producing unexpected and inexplicable results.

Interest rates have been near zero for six years, but businesses and individuals have not increased their overall borrowing. Corporate profits are high, but business is not booming. For example, stock prices often fall for companies that announce good earnings, while share values rise for companies that have lost big, just less than expected. The stabilizing function of free market capitalism has completely disappeared; the relatively few Americans who own capital are getting richer while the vast majority who provide labor are becoming poorer. Things are not making sense as they generally did in the twentieth century. The occasional light at the end of the tunnel is likely to be an oncoming train. (The US Commerce Department reduced its estimate of economic growth in 2013, from 3.2% to 2.4%, the day after I drafted this section. Supporting the observation that economic forces are not working as they once did, the stock market rose the following day.)

Increasing Demands from Other Sectors

The decline in continual, cumulative GDP growth is quickly shifting the country toward a zero-sum economy in which one economic unit can gain only at the expense of another. Consequently, many economists are struggling to revise macroeconomic models and policies for a steady-state (i.e., no-growth) economy in the postindustrial world. Within the constraints of little or no annual growth, markets must take from one sector to give to another, including trade-offs between health care and other important sectors of the economy (e.g., education, infrastructure, defense, housing, food). These other sectors desperately need resources and are fighting harder for their pieces of the fixed economic "pie." They will oppose any preferential treatment for health care because it will now be to their detriment. The tide that once raised all boats has disappeared.

Health care has also lost its historic position as most favored sector of the American economy—last to be cut and first to be restored in budget negotiations—because buyers have concluded that spending more on medical goods and services does not produce more health for the population. Why, American decision makers ask, should governments and employers continually allocate additional resources to health care if every comparable developed country can keep its people at least as healthy for 12% or less of the GDP instead of the 17% or more that we spend? Economic units on the demand side of the marketplace are done with paying more but not getting more. The accelerating shift from volume-based payment to value-based buying is most likely beyond the tipping point, which means organizations on the supply side will not be able to raise prices and quantity as they have in the past.

Constrained Consumer Spending

Governments and employers subsidized roughly 80% of all costs of medical care for several decades. Now they are not only making a typical patient responsible for any increases in spending, but are also ultimately increasing the patient's share above 20% as purchasers' shares fall below 80%. Employer-based health insurance has been accomplishing this shift over the past decade by increasing copayments and deductibles and by reducing covered benefits. Health insurance that covers almost all costs of care is a thing of the past for Americans under 65.

The Affordable Care Act (ACA) actually accelerates the shift by mandating purchase of policies priced to pay only 60% or 70% of a patient's expected costs of care. Specifically, the law's Silver and Bronze plans make insurance (not health care!) "affordable" by raising a patient's expected payment responsibility to 30% and 40% respectively—50% and 100% increases above the accustomed 20% out-of-pocket obligation. (A rise from 20% to 30% in consumer financial responsibility is a 50% increase; 20% to 40% is a doubling, or 100%, increase.) Forcing individual consumers to "have skin in the game" would not stop growth in spending if they had the money to pay more, but they do not. And, even if disposable per capita income starts growing again, there is no reason to believe consumers would spend it on health care. Historical experience suggests that extra cash would be spent on housing, transportation, education, food, and entertainment before it would go to health care.

As previously noted, there is also no guarantee that American consumers would spend additional income on health care in the United States. An increasing number of Americans now travel internationally to purchase health care in other countries, a relatively recent phenomenon known as medical tourism or medical travel. Providers in several foreign countries (e.g., India, Costa Rica, Thailand, Mexico), in collaboration with specialized travel agencies and American health insurance companies, are creating attractive opportunities for Americans to go abroad for medical services provided in Joint Commission-accredited hospitals by board-certified physicians who trained in the United States.

Significant reductions in federally funded medical research will also cause American providers to lose revenue to competitors in other countries, as will restrictive policies on stem cell research, genetic therapies, and visas for foreign scientists. Indeed, the restrictions have allowed several other countries to move ahead of the United States in some important domains of twenty-first-century medicine. Many American patients will therefore be going abroad not only to save money but also to obtain new treatments that are unavailable here. Finally, charitable foundations in the United States are expanding their financial support for health care projects in other countries. Health dollars that would have stayed in the United States in the past are leaving the country, further reducing health care's relative share of American GDP.

Increasing Diversification and Competition

Traditional providers and their main business partners—hospitals, physicians, health insurers, pharmaceutical companies, and medical equipment manufacturers—are rapidly losing the concentrated economic power that allowed them to ensure economic growth at the expense of other businesses throughout the second half of the twentieth century. Beyond the fact that purchasers are no longer able or willing to pay more for health care, the medical marketplace now offers a growing array of alternatives that were suppressed as long as medical care was controlled by professional guilds.

For reasons elaborated in my books, *Not What the Doctor Ordered* (1998) and *Telemedicine and the Reinvention of*

Health Care (1999),[1] organized medicine is no longer able to control hospitals or to prevent independent practice of qualified nonphysician caregivers, including nurse practitioners, certified registered nurse anesthetists, certified nurse midwives, physical therapists and clinical pharmacists with doctoral degrees. Public acceptance of these highly trained professionals has allowed pharmacy chains and innovative entrepreneurs to compete directly for the limited dollars spent on health care. Telecommunications and information technologies (e.g., telemedicine, mobile health) have also enabled the rapid development of new care mechanisms that overcome the long-standing barriers of place and time.

Consumerism is another major dimension of the increasing competition for pieces of the fixed health care pie. Both public and private reforms are significantly increasing individuals' direct involvement in deciding what to buy and how much to pay in the medical marketplace. Evidence already suggests that a growing number of patients do not want high-cost treatments when they perceive that minimal benefits and painful side effects are not worth the financial burden. Purchasers, health plans, consumer groups, and the media are all working to make consumers more aware of choices and prices. The bottom-line goal of consumerism is to reduce spending on health care, creating one more way that total expenditures are being capped. Consumerism will continue to develop unevenly over the next few years, but its impact on the medical marketplace will grow. Providers are rapidly moving from the comfort of price making to the stress of price taking, another force bringing an end to growth in health spending.

Improvement in Scientific Indications for Medical Care

The workings of the medical marketplace are usually analyzed from the perspective of economic theory. However, changes in the quantity of goods and services consumed over time are not determined solely by price, and economic analysis alone does not encompass one of the most important determinants of demand for medical care: the scientific foundations of good clinical practice. This is a serious shortcoming because medical science is starting to play a significant role in curbing consumption for sound scientific reasons. By extension, growing adherence to emerging principles of good clinical practice will likely limit the portion of GDP allocated to health care.

Having spent almost half my more than 40-year career as a statistics and research professor in academic health centers and the remainder as a medical economist and health futurist working with community hospitals and medical groups, I believe that revolutionary new knowledge of human health will impact the medical marketplace at least as much as economic and political forces. Physicians and other qualified caregivers deserve recognition for intensifying their commitment to evidence-based practices that will reduce demand for care, independent of economic considerations. More medical leaders are taking moves to stop providing services that cannot reasonably be expected to improve outcomes—even when they lose income in the process. Indeed, several medical specialties (e.g., radiology, urology, oncology, internal medicine) have recently taken strong positions to halt unnecessary demand for their services. Choosing Wisely (http://www.choosingwisely.org) is an excellent example of collective professional action to eliminate wasteful care.

The Hippocratic Oath has dictated for nearly 2,500 years that monetary considerations should never influence a doctor's decisions on what is best for each patient—a promise physicians could easily keep because they controlled health insurance until relatively late in the twentieth century. Insurance paid whatever was billed, allowing physicians to base treatment decisions on their own experience and judgment. Managed care tried to limit demand in the 1990s through the use of gatekeepers, but physicians uniformly resisted its limitations on their independence until "big data" started to guide clinical decision making in the 2000s. Government agencies and academic researchers suddenly had analytical capabilities to identify clinical interventions that did not improve patients' health, regardless of their cost. Physicians can be expected to fight bureaucratic gatekeepers, but nearly all will ultimately change their practice patterns in response to data that define standards of practice at a national level.

Large databases are already reducing health expenditures by identifying procedures and drugs that do not contribute to the health of populations. Rapidly advancing knowledge of illnesses at the molecular level goes a step further by determining if an intervention can be expected to benefit a specific individual. This new concept of care, known as precision medicine, will have a significant economic impact by targeting therapies only to patients who can be expected to benefit from them. Consequently, the overall use of medical goods and services will decline because data will identify interventions that are not beneficial, and in many cases, even harmful, for populations and individuals.

These new capabilities to analyze clinical data and inform clinical decision making will bring an end to unchecked growth in health care spending and its share of GDP. Physicians and other qualified caregivers will be generating less demand for clinical reasons, regardless of the medical marketplace's economic characteristics and financial incentives. Even the long-standing argument against this effect, malpractice liability, will diminish significantly as physicians have good data to show that defensive medicine is not only unnecessary, but often harmful. We are not far from the day when a physician is as likely to be held liable for harm resulting from an unnecessary test as for a diagnosis missed because a necessary test was not performed. The demand for health services will fall, even if malpractice law is not reformed, as mounting scientific evidence shows that risks outweigh benefits for many common tests and procedures.

The More Things Change

Convergence of these five factors will generate even more structural change in the medical marketplace as the "new normals" continue to displace traditional forces that allowed medical care to grow relatively faster than other sectors throughout the second half of the twentieth century. My views as medical economist and health futurist therefore lead to the following conclusion: *Health care spending has peaked at current levels in relative terms, around 17% of GDP.* Health care's portion of all final economic activity in the United States has quit growing; the medical marketplace is no longer an engine of growth.

This jarring conclusion is already supported by information from the Centers for Medicare and Medicaid Services (CMS). According to its March 2014 summary of National Health Expenditure (NHE) data,[2] health spending in the United States increased by 3.7% between 2011 and 2012 while GDP increased 4.6%, causing the health-spending share of the economy to decrease from 17.3% to 17.2% of GDP over the same period. The peak of 17.4% was hit in 2009 and 2010, up from 16.4% in 2008.

Because the CMS report noted that the previously estimated value for 2012 was 17.9% and included an earlier projection of 19.6% for 2021, many will simply assume the decline is a short-term deviation from the long-term path of "unsustainable" growth. I believe subsequent NHE reports will most likely prove them wrong. Given the substantial time lag in government economic data, the end of growth in medical spending around 17% of GDP will not be widely recognized as the long-term (i.e., multiyear) trend—the new normal—until preliminary figures for 2014 are issued in 2016 and final figures are issued sometime in 2017.

Long delays in availability of final data—not to mention extremely serious deficiencies in reliability (accuracy) and validity (meaningfulness) of the published numbers—deserve a lot more attention than they receive. As noted in the preceding discussion, key factors that determine the health system's performance are changing at a rapid, accelerating pace. I am one of many observers who believe that the half-life of today's information about health care is less than two years; at least 50% of the variables measured by government data will have new and meaningfully different values by the time official reports are published two or more years after the data were collected. Hence, the common practice of evaluating today's medical marketplace with the most recently published (i.e., two-year-old) data is likely to be half wrong at the outset, and prospective projections based on today's data will miss the mark by an equal or greater margin because of the increasing rate of change over time.

Due to the new forces that are redefining the medical marketplace, health care providers and their business partners should not expect to obtain a disproportionately larger share of GDP even if the nation's economic growth returns to pre-2008 levels. Anyone whose future is tied to health care should act accordingly. Past performance is no longer an indicator of future results, as shown previously by the downward correction in the 2012 data from an initial estimate of 17.9% to a final figure of 17.2%. Providers can no longer stay in business simply by raising prices or increasing volume for goods and services at the expense of other sectors, and investors should stop describing the health sector as "bulletproof." The medical marketplace is no longer immune from the overall economy's ups and downs, a compelling reason to approach the future of American health care in a new and different way.

We should also remember that health care's growth from 4.5% of GDP in 1960 to its maximum of 17.4% in 2010 did not produce corresponding increases in the health of Americans compared to their counterparts in other countries. To be clear, medical science and health professionals produced remarkable improvements in care and cure over the past 50 years, but population health in other developed countries stayed ahead of the United States over the same period, without comparable increases in medical spending. Consequently, the taxpayers, employers, and consumers who pay providers' bills have learned that spending more is not necessarily a good thing. It does not make the American population healthier. They are fed up with changing (i.e., increasing) their expenditures on a system that does not change (i.e., improve).

As a Francophile, I am reminded of a familiar aphorism that aptly describes our medical marketplace from this point forward, albeit with a new twist in meaning: The more health care delivery changes, the more health care spending stays the same. Another common French saying, about the need to break eggs to make an omelet, is also appropriate. Other culinary analogies are equally to the point when it comes to American health care. We are finally realizing that we cannot eat our cake and have it, too, in the medical marketplace. Our traditional approach to health reform is holding out for pie in the sky.

The Bottom Line: Redirecting Reform

ObamaCare's defenders cannot fairly claim that the law is responsible for ending the growth in medical spending. The new normal forces were taking shape well before the ACA was passed, and the law's centerpiece—an individual mandate to purchase health insurance—played no role in development of the new marketplace dynamics. Substantive, accumulating delays in implementing the law further undermine any claims that it has reduced spending. Even the law's most fervent supporter (Speaker of the House Nancy Pelosi) admitted when the law was passed that she did not know what was in it, and one of its most vocal detractors (former Speaker Newt Gingrich) pointed out that the law had not been read by anyone who voted for it. It is therefore disingenuous for reform leaders who did not know what the law would do to claim credit for whatever it has done, good or bad.

The reform law's primary goal, expanding the number of Americans with health insurance, is not a wise use of scarce resources in a failed marketplace. Regardless of the intent of the ACA's creators, the following chapters show why and how the key to success in a no-growth sector is efficient and effective management of scarce resources. The end of growth in medical spending provides the compelling imperative for rebuilding an economic sector that is broken from top to bottom. The focus of marketplace reform needs to be redirected, expeditiously and purposefully, to waste-free production of health care of expected and acceptable quality. Creating a good medical care delivery system should replace expanding access to the existing system as the top priority of health reform.

The payment-focused, implementation-challenged ACA of 2010 is a classic case of putting the cart before the horse. It simply cannot lead to top-quality, least-cost care for all Americans in an economic sector that has quit growing. Because we have hit the limits of spending on health care, we must realistically accept the need to make choices and trade-offs. We must develop a new approach to reform reflecting the fact that only one variable can be optimized (e.g., quality maximized *or* cost minimized *or* access for all) when resources are fixed. Because more money will not be available to do more things, our politicians and policy makers must quit making promises that cannot be kept and imposing programs that will not work.

Consequently, America's long-standing approach to health reform—one-size-fits-all federal laws and regulations intended to create highest-quality and lowest-cost care for all—must be abandoned. The three goals cannot be met all at once under current or foreseeable economic circumstances. One goal at a time must be selected as the top priority if reform is ever to be worth the resources and effort it consumes. Building on health professionals' primary obligation to do no harm, I propose maximizing quality as the guiding principle for Democratic efforts to repair ObamaCare or Republican efforts to replace it. The new mantra of reform should be *providing health care appropriately all the time, as inexpensively as possible.* I hope this book will generate bipartisan support for redirecting reform accordingly.

The good news, I firmly believe, is that enough leaders on the supply side of the medical marketplace have the required knowledge and professional commitment to provide care of consistent, expected quality if reform laws were changed to allow them to focus their efforts on achieving one goal at a time. Sequenced, accountable steps toward a specific goal would be much better than today's unrealistic, unfocused approach forcing providers and payers to address so many problems simultaneously that they cannot adequately respond to any of them.

Resources saved by eliminating unproductive or defective medical services can be subsequently reallocated to expanding access, shifted as quickly as possible to improving the health of all Americans under a redirected approach to health reform. Long-term public policy should be simultaneously formulated to preserve the medical economy at 17% of GDP to ensure that money saved through elimination of waste is available for expanding access to least-expensive, appropriate services. The remainder of this book presents economic and strategic analysis for this redirected approach to reform; including three specific policies for making it happen.

Problems with Predicting the Future of Health Care

I did not need to gaze into a crystal ball to see that historical growth in health care spending, relative to overall economic activity, is coming to an end. It is the current situation; no futurism is required. Government data are already consistent with no relative growth, and the five new normal forces discussed above are aligning to prevent disproportional expansion of the medical economy for the foreseeable future. To be clear, current trends suggest total spending on health care will continue to increase, but not at a greater rate than increases in GDP.

Confusion on the spending-GDP relationship in health care is common, as is confusion on the difference between prices and spending. Total spending on a good or service stays the same when prices rise and demand falls proportionally; an increase in prices does not mean an increase in total spending in this situation. I expect this general relationship, falling demand in response to higher out-of-pocket prices, will quickly become another new normal in the medical marketplace. Recent evidence suggests that patients are already reducing their demand for medical care in response to increases in the prices they must pay.

A few more years of data will be needed before we medical economists can draw a conclusion about the relationship between price and demand, and that conclusion will be tentative. Evaluating the real price of health care is becoming increasingly difficult. Providers have a list price for all their goods and services, called the charge master price. It is usually listed on the bill, but almost no one (except patients without insurance) is expected to pay it. Insurance companies pay lower amounts based on discounts, or "contractual allowances," and different insurers have negotiated a wide range of discounts. In other words, many different prices are paid for the same billed item.

The price generally paid by an individual patient is the deductible amount and then the coinsurance rate on any remaining balance. However, patients are increasingly requesting and receiving reductions in their bills, so the actual price paid for a given good or service is almost impossible to determine. The issue is further complicated by the price a patient paid for health insurance; it is not allocated to any particular purchase, but it definitely influences demand. (When speaking about this subject, I tell audiences they only understand medical pricing if they are confused by it.) Economists will need to be careful when they start drawing conclusions about the impact of prices, especially with the complications introduced by the ACA.

The end of growth in medical spending with respect to the rest of the economy will come as a surprise to many readers because the Democrats' relentless push for health reform in 2009 and 2010 was driven by a well-publicized prediction that health care would be 20% of GDP in 2015, not 17% (see Figure 1.1). The ACA was pushed through a divided Congress on the grounds that the situation would be even worse than predicted if the law were not passed. According to the ACA's creators, the cost curve absolutely had to be "bent" to prevent it from rising above 20%.

The dramatic discrepancy between a prediction made in 2009 and reality five years later underscores a serious problem with making a prediction, the mathematical process of estimating a future value of a key variable. For reasons I have explained in *Upgrading Leadership's Crystal Ball: Five Reasons Why Forecasting Must Replace Predicting and How to Make the Strategic Change in Business and Public Policy* (2014),[3] predictions are irrelevant in any economic sector when causality is being redefined. Predictions are only valid in systems in which the quantifiable relationships that represented how

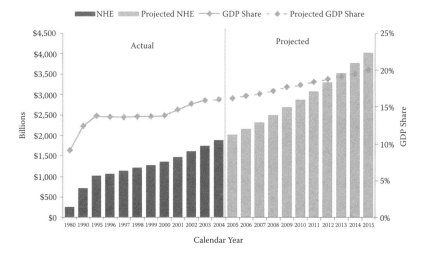

National Health Expenditures and Their Share of Gross Domestic Product (GDP), 1980-2015

National health spending is projected to continue to increase as a share of GDP over the next decade.

Source: CMS, Office of the Actuary, National Health Statistics Group.

Figure 1.1   Erroneous prediction of continued growth in health care expenditures.

things worked in the past will continue to work the same way in the future—decidedly not the situation in health care today. As stated at the outset of this chapter, the medical marketplace is currently in a state of chaos, and new normal factors have replaced those that prevailed for several decades until this one. American health care's future is literally unpredictable under such circumstances.

Even if a system's causal relationships are not changing, predictions are almost always wrong for a variety of additional reasons, including unreliable (i.e., inaccurate) and invalid (i.e., unrepresentative) data, plus fatal discrepancies between assumptions about the system's dynamics and assumptions about the predictive model being used to project a future state. These violations of fundamental principles are especially problematic in health care today, providing one more reason not to use predictions for designing strategies to improve the health care delivery system and the medical marketplace. Today's policy makers should quit worrying about health spending in the future and start defining the best ways to spend 17% of GDP on health care right now.

Medical Professionalism and Solving Economic Problems

My observations on today's medical marketplace and its future must be placed in proper theoretical perspective. Parson Malthus' well-known characterization of economics as the "dismal" science—dismal because he believed unchecked natural forces inevitably lead to famine and misery—gives a misleading impression of the importance of economic analysis in chaotic times. Fortunately, post-Malthusian economics evolved to pursue more desirable outcomes with policies to redirect natural tendencies. Good economists now use theory to craft incentives for shaping better outcomes. Economists must nevertheless dig into dismal problems to propose acceptable ways to solve them. They also understand the necessity of trade-offs and how to guide difficult choices in the process of solving problems.

As an economist, my goal for this book is to analyze health care from a positive perspective, contradicting conventional wisdom about health care as a failed market. Further, as a teacher and consultant proud of working for 45 years with medical professionals who swear above all else to do no harm, my goal is to recommend policies that do no harm *even if I am wrong in concluding that the medical marketplace has quit growing*. All health professionals should be putting top priority on efficiency and effectiveness. They should not be changing the ways they do business simply because economic circumstances have suddenly deteriorated.

Rather, providers and their business partners should change the way they do business simply because it is the right thing to do for the patients they serve. Preventing the personal and economic harms of substandard medical care is the modern expression of the first principle of professionalism in medicine. By extension, I suggest that doing no harm should also be the first principle of health reform—the absolute precondition for ultimately providing all Americans with the best health care that 17% of GDP can buy.

This goal is much more realistic than politically popular but economically impossible "reforms" to provide the best possible care to all Americans for less money. Indeed, believing that health care deserves more than 17% of GDP is disrespectful of other essential attributes of a just society. Health care leaders have not thought enough about how their rising claim on limited resources deprives Americans of other equally defensible rights, such as education, food and shelter, safety, and so on. The economic concept of opportunity costs should be at the forefront of policy discussions.

In addition to honoring the fundamental professional obligation to do no harm, leaders in the business of health care must purposefully change their ways because enormous waste—measured in cost *and* quality—has finally become unacceptable to the people who pay the bills. Purchasers, payers, and patients all believe that inefficient and ineffective approaches to health care delivery should be eliminated. If dramatic changes are not soon made by stakeholders with power to improve health care from within, outsiders are likely to impose solutions even more damaging than the end of economic growth in the medical marketplace. Failure of professionalism could ultimately lead to a single payer in the United States at a time when most other countries are moving in the opposite direction.

Fortunately, chaos need not foretell a dismal future. Good outcomes have often arisen from disorganized, unpredictable situations throughout history. Visionary leaders who develop and implement responsive new strategies for the right professional reason not only can survive but also can thrive. They will end the paradox of a second-rate health system in the world's number one economy by responding to the economic, clinical, and professional imperatives of a new medical marketplace. Professional pride alone should motivate the country's health care leaders to put top priority on becoming efficient and effective in order to liberate resources for expanding access, as discussed in the following chapters. Only then can the United States legitimately lay global claim to having the world's best health care system.

Notes

1. Jeffrey C. Bauer. *Not What the Doctor Ordered.* New York: McGraw-Hill, 1998; and Jeffrey C. Bauer and Marc C. Ringel. *Telemedicine and the Reinvention of Health Care.* New York: McGraw-Hill, 1999.
2. For NHE details, see http://www.cms.gov/Research-Statistics-Data-and-Systems/Statistics-Trends-and-Reports/NationalHealthExpendData/NHE-Fact-Sheet.html.
3. Jeffrey C. Bauer. *Upgrading Leadership's Crystal Ball: Five Reasons Why Forecasting Must Replace Predicting and How to Make the Strategic Change in Business and Public Policy.* Boca Raton, FL: CRC Press, 2014.

Chapter 3

The Economic Imperative: Efficiency (Cost)

Introduction

Health care is not the first American industry for which producers had to reinvent their way of doing business in order to survive. Indeed, it may be among the last to respond creatively to the economic upheavals that mark the new millennium. Dramatic changes in the marketplace have forced almost every other sector of the economy to restructure its operations over the past two decades. Today's leading airlines, banks, accounting firms, manufacturers, information processors, news and entertainment conglomerates, insurers, retailers, and energy distributors bear little resemblance to the companies that dominated their respective industries in the 1980s and 1990s. Many businesses changed their names to reflect major reorganization and reorientation. Others kept their well-established corporate identities but shifted to very different business models, value propositions, distribution chains, and customer relations.

Basic principles of economics are behind the successful, *enduring* transformations in other industries. Some infamous enterprises (e.g., Enron, WorldCom) used noneconomic methods to grow impressively for a while, but good investigative reporters and dedicated federal prosecutors ultimately ended the run of companies that resorted to fraud and greed. Exploiting loopholes in regulations and otherwise gaming the system are temporary solutions at best and crimes at worst. Following good business practices while innovating is the reliable way to stay in business. My analysis and recommendations therefore assume that successful health care providers will transform legally and professionally.

Ethical managers who have successfully met the challenges of change in nonhealth industries consistently return to basic principles taught in Economics 101, even though the basic concepts often receive new names over time. The innovators examine every aspect of producing and selling their product, constantly pursuing ways to do things differently because business as usual is not a promising option when the world of business is being transformed. One universal ingredient in the "secret sauce" of successful economic adoption in chaotic times is operational awareness of the time frames in which changes can be made within the industry.

Short Run versus Long Run

Basic concepts of economics are often forgotten, probably because they are poorly taught at the introductory level and never truly understood. Consequently, discussion of successful transformation in health care begins with a quick review of one of the key concepts of economic analysis: the difference between short-run and long-run perspectives. Health care executives and medical leaders must incorporate this difference in their thinking and decision making as they respond to new opportunities in the medical marketplace.

As we economists say, with our proclivity for understatement, the difference between the short run and the long run is not trivial. Successful executives see the need for short-run *and* long-run solutions to problems that are threatening the enterprise. They coordinate the two perspectives as distinctly different tasks because inquests into business failures often find that managers were focused on one perspective at the expense of the other. Although this book is decidedly focused on long-run analysis, it does not diminish the importance of attention to the short run. Ongoing survival requires both perspectives.

Neither time frame is defined in economic analysis as a specific interval on a calendar. Measuring the short run as one or two years and the long run as three to five years is a common practice, but it misses a critical distinction with respect to decision making.

- The **short run** is the period when inputs cannot be changed. The manager's task is to find the best combination of existing inputs (e.g., employees on the payroll, supplies in the stockroom) to produce a desired good or service. The quantities of all resources are fixed in the short run. The only approach to improved performance is trying different combinations of the resources at hand.
- The **long run** begins when all inputs can be changed. The manager's task in the long run is to evaluate alternative combinations of inputs and to make trade-offs that will produce better goods and services. Because all resources are variable in the long run, existing resources can be reallocated to different uses or be replaced with new ones to align an organization's future with changes in the marketplace.

Leaders who successfully transformed other industries have bridged the gap between short-run and long-run thinking. After fine-tuning the interaction of existing inputs to address current problems, they learned how to rethink products and production processes in the context of uncertainty and change. They envisioned not only different ways to run the day-to-day businesses, but also the possibility of doing new things that had good prospects for success once they had negotiated the necessary trade-offs: selling a division, developing a new product, reengineering a process, adopting a new technology, retraining employees, outsourcing a business function, creating a partnership (sometimes with a competitor), and so on.

Health care executives need to accomplish the same transition to shape desirable futures for their enterprises. Responding to the medical marketplace's new imperatives requires long-run thinking open to the possibility that anything and everything can be changed. Tasks can be reassigned to new personnel. Procedures can be revised. Space can be remodeled to serve different purposes. Hospitals and physicians can work for the same economic unit. Traditional service lines can be discontinued, allowing specialization in a market niche or moves into a new one. In operational terms, the ability to identify feasible alternatives and make responsive changes is a critical success factor when total spending has peaked. Managing solely for the short run was viable when health care was growing relative to the rest of the economy, but those days are gone.

Tactics versus Strategy

Academic observers have said that professors in economics departments and business schools generally teach the same concepts but occasionally give them different names. Economists and their business school counterparts tend to be consistent in explanations of the short run and long run, but my experience suggests confusion on the related distinction between tactics and strategy. Treating them as synonyms can obscure an important difference in operational application of the two concepts.

- **Tactics** involve the realm of management skills necessary for dealing with the short run. Chief operating officers and their department heads need to be tacticians. They work with limited budgets (i.e., fixed resources) that define the personnel and materials available for doing a specific job in a fixed period of time. They are responsible for finding the best combination of resources at hand to do the job that needs to be done now.
- **Strategy** is the realm of long-run skills needed for structuring proactive, enterprise-wide responses to anticipated changes in the marketplace. The chief executive officer is responsible for strategy (in collaboration with the board of directors, according to good governance practice), with the ability to delegate tactical authority to trusted and talented subordinates. Chief executives need to be long-run thinkers who explore alternatives within and across departments. They need to have the skills *and courage* to reallocate internal resources to achieve better outcomes, including major changes in product mix, in response to meaningful trends in the marketplace.

Business school professors use a variety of examples to illustrate the operationally meaningful difference between tactics and strategy. In sports, for example, coaches are the tacticians because they must try to win with the players who suited up for each game. Team owners and general managers are the strategists who decide whether to make trades or hire a new coach so that future games will be played differently. In the military, lieutenants are the tacticians responsible for fighting with the troops and armaments that are on the field for a given battle. Generals make strategic decisions away from the battlefield, such as shifting resources between naval, air, and ground troops. Their reallocations will change the way future battles are fought.

Key to Success: Long-Run Strategy

Given the marketplace's new imperatives, health care's leaders must be good long-run strategists. They need the intellectual skills to explore possible combinations of an expanded array of factors of production—identified and discussed in the following pages—and the leadership skills to motivate stakeholders to move cooperatively in new directions. Their goals will be to cut the waste out of the medical marketplace and then to reallocate recovered resources to improving population health. Their decisions and actions will reflect an often-quoted but seldom honored maxim: If getting what you have always gotten is not working, quit doing what you have always done.

Although this book explores many facets of future-focused change, it assumes that applying the principles of long-run strategy is still a challenge for the leaders of many provider organizations and their business partners. The historical norm in health care is trying to preserve business as usual. Many trustees, senior executives, and clinical leaders do not want to assume the responsibilities and risks of being a long-run strategist. For a variety of reasons, intentional and unintentional, they choose not to rock the boat. They are dedicated and honorable people, but they are not interested in breaking eggs or leading a revolution.

Why protect the status quo? Most health care leaders do not want to experience the predictably unpleasant consequences of terminating a marginal service line, assigning employees to unfamiliar tasks, confronting a recalcitrant member of the medical staff, collaborating with a perceived adversary, or standing up to a regulatory agency. Managing by conflict avoidance was generally not fatal to the health care enterprise when purchasers and payers could ultimately be counted on to pay the high costs of the resulting inefficiencies.

However, as demonstrated in the previous chapter, purchasers and their third-party agents are no longer able or willing to subsidize waste in health care. And, consumers definitely do not have disposable income to pay their rising share of the bill for services that they believe are overpriced for the value received. Unless providers have a generous and forgiving benefactor, a large and unrestricted endowment, or exceptional market power, they must implement strategies for long-run change in the way they produce their services. They must control operating costs because they cannot increase net revenue through traditional means. In a word, providers must become efficient.

Need for Common Understanding

Imagine a pop quiz in which health care leaders, politicians, and policy analysts are asked to define *efficiency* in economic terms and then to describe a process for improving the efficiency of a medical service. My experience suggests that the answers would be highly variable and generally imprecise. This inconsistency points to a serious problem: The health industry is not efficient because most of its leaders do not have a clear understanding of efficiency and efficient production processes.

The problem is so pervasive and its consequences so expensive that correcting it is an essential precondition for meaningful improvements in the American health care delivery system. The current approach to health reform is focused almost exclusively on meeting the needs of the uninsured, but inefficiency is the elephant in the living room that everyone ignores. Even if all Americans were to obtain health insurance, the United States would still have an unaffordable health care system as long as providers and their business partners lack the knowledge, authority, responsibility, and incentives to become efficient.

Consequently, a common operational understanding of efficiency must be created across the industry as a precondition for providing appropriate health care of acceptable quality as inexpensively as possible. Real progress toward the three goals of health reform cannot occur until "everyone is reading off the same page." The good news is that economists (and management engineers, who apply the same principles) have a standardized definition of efficiency and a common set of quantitative tools for determining the most efficient combination of resources needed to produce a specific good or service. Their concept of efficiency is, metaphorically speaking, an excellent page from which all should be reading.

As promised in the Preface, I will not dwell on economic theory any more than necessary to make it strategically useful to senior executives and their boards. This section tells leaders what they need to know to articulate and implement strategies for becoming efficient. The nitty-gritty tasks of implementing strategies should be delegated to managers and consultants who have spent years learning and using the tools of the efficiency trade. Leaders responsible for their organization's future only need to understand the fundamental concepts and why efficiency is quickly becoming essential to the success of their organizations. The strategists do not need to know how to operationalize efficiency, but they must become champions of efficiency and know how to judge the work of their tactical managers who have day-to-day responsibility for identifying wasted resources and making the recovered resources available for the subsequent accomplishment of strategic goals.

Efficiency for Executives

In the theory of economics and management engineering, *efficiency* is defined in two different, but equivalent, ways:

■ **Maximum output for a fixed budget**: An outcome for which managers are using the combination of inputs that produces the greatest quantity of a specific good or service for a given amount of money (e.g., finding the combination of nurses, physicians, treatment spaces, supplies, and technologies that yields the maximum number of annual visits to an emergency department (ED) for an annual operating budget of $5 million). From this perspective, efficiency is the highest output of a specific product that you can produce for a fixed number of dollars.

or

■ **Minimum cost for a fixed output**: An outcome for which managers have used the combination of inputs that produces a fixed quantity of a specific good or service at the least-expensive cost (e.g., finding the lowest budget for covering the cost of nurses, physicians, treatment spaces, supplies, and technologies needed to produce 50,000 annual visits to an ED). From this perspective, efficiency is the minimum number of dollars needed to meet a predetermined production goal.

Most people are surprised that one question can require two answers to be correct. This uncommon duality would partly explain the wide variation in answers to the hypothetical pop test question. Nearly everyone would provide only one answer, which means that nearly everyone would be half-right at best. Ironically, I expect the most common answer on my hypothetical pop quiz would be that efficiency is producing as much as possible for the lowest cost. This answer is not only wrong but also impossible when resources are fixed. Even more surprising, the two answers seem to be very different, but in reality, they are only different ways to describe the same point—the bottoms of various configurations of the U-shaped cost curves that everyone studied in Economics 101.

To honor my promise to tell leaders only what they need to know, I have intentionally (maybe even mercifully?) decided not to clutter this book with several pages of U-shaped cost curves and explanations of production functions. Anyone who really wants a refresher can obtain it from a basic economics textbook, but I do not think that a health care executive is ever going to move his or her organization forward using U-shaped cost curves in motivational presentations to stake-holders and managers. Besides, assuming that executives have hired qualified managers, the experts who actually do the work will already know the concepts and mathematics of effi-cient production.

Executives need to know that efficient production can be achieved in one of two different ways: minimizing costs for a predetermined output *or* maximizing output for a predeter-mined budget. They must hold their managers accountable for accomplishing one of them. If the organization does not have sufficient resources to do either one, something in the process must be reduced (e.g., fewer services, lower quality) when resources cannot be increased. The traditional response of raising prices without changing the production process is not viable in today's medical marketplace. Further, reducing qual-ity is not acceptable if providing health care appropriately all the time is the first step in the redirected approach to reform.

Problems to Avoid

Three serious mistakes are commonly made in pursuit of effi-ciency. To avoid one or more of these traps, leaders of health care delivery organizations must understand the potential pitfalls of efficiency and communicate them to line managers who are responsible for translating long-run strategy into daily practice. If there were going to be a pop quiz at the end of this chapter, the exam would definitely include questions on all three points.

■ First, efficiency in any production unit (e.g., a specialty department, a hospital service line) can be pursued one way *or* the other, but not both ways in today's medical marketplace. As already noted, a very common mistake is defining efficiency as the greatest output for the least cost. The coexistence of a maximum (greatest output) and a minimum (least cost) in a closed system is technically impossible. As executives should have learned in their quantitative methods courses, only one variable can be maximized or minimized in a system with limited (i.e., fixed) resources: the market situation that health care is now entering. Other factors can serve as constraints (i.e., fixed limits on the values of key parameters), which is why efficiency is defined either as cost minimization for a fixed output or output maximization for a fixed cost. In engineering science, the general model for finding an efficient outcome is known as constrained optimization.

■ Second, managers must be told or allowed to decide which of these two paths to follow in pursuit of an efficient outcome for their departments or service lines. Production units are often told to produce more for less, a dictum that almost always promotes inefficiency because it does not force managers to focus on doing one thing as well as possible. Instead, they should start with an output objective, such as the number of services to be provided in a unit or an annual budget. Department heads, with support of efficiency experts as needed, should then evaluate different input combinations that would minimize cost to meet the fixed output goal or maximize output to stay within the fixed budget. Output maximization is not inherently better than cost minimization or vice versa. The enterprise's financial status and competitive situation will usually suggest which approach to take, with the possibility of case-by-case differences. The senior executive's task is to make sure that line managers are focused on one approach or the other, not both, when they adopt efficiency as a core organizational value.

■ Third, efficiency is a moving target in health care. Holding steadfastly to an efficient outcome can be counterproductive over time. Scientific advances are forcing new clinical demands on providers faster than ever before, and new technologies are constantly expanding the realm of possibilities for maximizing outputs or minimizing costs in the delivery of health services. A combination of professionals, equipment, and space that is efficient today could quickly become inefficient on the publication of new clinical evidence, introduction of better technology, or a change in the payment for care. Rapidity of change reinforces the compelling need for executives to take a long-run strategic view of their enterprises. They must propagate the view that all resources are variable and ensure that appropriate trade-offs are constantly made within their enterprises. Measurable movement in the direction of efficiency is generally the best that can be expected in an industry that is being constantly changed by science, technology, demographics, and economics—such as health care.

The rapidity of change in medical science and technology deserves special consideration in the current context of government-driven health reform. The ACA includes several demonstration programs to test different proposals for reducing costs or increasing supply of medical services. (Several of the approaches being tested were featured as case studies in the first edition of this book.) ObamaCare's proponents contend that the demonstration programs will ultimately generate operational efficiencies to bend the cost curve—the reform goal that fell by the wayside when insurance expansion and payment reform became the focus of last-minute politics to get the legislation passed.

As is typical of federal demonstration programs, the process of setting up regulations and bureaucracies to oversee the demonstrations usually takes a year or two, and then the actual demonstrations are conducted for three or four years. The final, highly politicized (i.e., not scientific) tasks of analyzing data, writing reports, and making recommendations take at least another year before policy makers decide whether and how to convert demonstrations into universal programs.

Given this cumbersome process, a former director of the Center for Medicare and Medicaid Services has observed that federal demonstration projects have never had any long-term impact on the delivery of health care. Further, the ACA specifically prevents federal health programs from using results of demonstration programs to reduce program benefits. Medicare and Medicaid are forbidden from adopting features of demonstration projects that reduce demand for services—an irrational restriction in an era of health reform.

Politics aside, the five- to seven-year, start-to-finish cycle of demonstration programs creates problems because medical services are advancing at a much faster rate. Current concepts of clinical care, including best practices, are often outmoded within a few years because of the rapidity of advances in science, technology, and analytics. ACA-driven (i.e., politically based) demonstration programs simply cannot keep up under the circumstances. They may be well intentioned, but they are inherently inefficient (i.e., wasteful) in a sector that is changing but not growing.

Inefficiency Equals Waste

One word links the theoretical concept of efficiency to the economic reality of health care: *waste*. This single word says as much as all the economic equations used to prove the point. Further, efficiency and waste are inversely related; efficiency increases as waste decreases and vice versa. A 100%

efficient system is waste free. No resource going into the process could be reallocated to a more productive use; every input is being optimally employed. In a 100% inefficient system, scarce resources go in and nothing of value comes out; every single input could be put to better use.

Another very important correlate of waste is *opportunity costs*—the other things that could be produced with the same resources. This book is effectively an inquiry into the opportunity costs of the way we have been spending our health care dollars for the past several decades. From my economist's perspective, the high number of Americans without health insurance is an opportunity cost of the abundant waste in the way health services are produced and financed in the United States. The process of redirecting reform should focus on managing the shift in resources from one use to another, that is, the shift from waste to a healthier population.

Economists, engineers, and other efficiency experts define waste as resources consumed in excess of those needed to minimize costs of a specified output *or* to maximize output for a specified budget. To extend the previous example of this bipartite definition, assume a management engineering study determines that a maximum of 50,000 visits of acceptable quality could be provided in a particular hospital's ED for an annual budget of $4 million. There is a waste of $1 million if the hospital is actually spending $5 million to deliver 50,000 ED visits. The opportunity cost is the other goods and services that could be produced with the wasted million dollars, such as providing more ED visits, transferring the funds to a different department where additional resources will be productive, or ultimately (i.e., once we have built an efficient and effective health care system) using the money to provide appropriate care for patients who do not have the financial ability to pay for it.

The wasted $1 million might include money spent on overstaffing that causes caregivers to get in each other's way (diminishing returns, in economic terms). It could be the cumulative cost of $100-an-hour physicians waiting a minute here and minute there for $15-an-hour technicians to assist with procedures or the salaries of several clerks who are needed to keyboard information on paper forms into electronic databases. Drug administration errors could account for part of the wasted million, as would the cost of redundant diagnostic tests to obtain information that was already in a patient's medical record—inaccessibly located elsewhere in the hospital.

Waste might also include money spent on duplicative diagnostics, in which a radiologist or a pathologist repeats a review of test results interpreted hours earlier by an ED physician. From the perspective of an efficiency expert, it could also be the cost of supplies discarded because they were stored beyond the expiration date or opened but not used. Waste could even be the money spent to build more ED treatment areas because housekeepers are not always available to clean bays as soon as patients are transferred elsewhere or the purchase of another imaging device when the existing one could be used for longer hours.

From the perspective of efficiency's other definition, imagine a situation in which 40,000 annual visits to an ED are being produced with the same production bottlenecks at a cost of $4 million per year. If improvements in space utilization, materials management, employee scheduling, and other process improvements could increase the service's capabilities up to 50,000 visits without increasing the annual budget, the ED has been sacrificing the 10,000 visits that could have been delivered but were not. Spending another $1 million to add 10,000 visits would be a waste when the same increase in volume could instead be achieved by management reengineering at no extra cost.

Comparable examples of inefficiency exist across the board in almost all provider organizations. To avoid the intellectual inefficiency of paralysis by analysis, I have avoided the temptation to pad this chapter with a large number of specific examples of waste. (Believe me, I could provide hundreds.)

Readers will understand the general point: The supply side of the medical marketplace is inefficient. If providers want to continue meeting the demands for health care, they must capture and reallocate wasted resources to productive use because the people who foot the bill are not going to pay any more in the future than they have in the past. The old days of compensating for inefficiency with more money are gone. Provider organizations that do not understand this point also will be gone.

Enough Waste to Matter?

Will the costs of eliminating waste exceed the money saved in the process? Is there enough waste in American health care to justify redirecting reform's goals from expanding insurance coverage to reallocating unproductive resources? Will building an efficient health system over the next few years liberate enough resources to expand access thereafter? The answers to these questions are critically important. Putting efficiency first would be wasteful in itself if it costs more than it saves or if it saves so little that few uninsured Americans would ultimately benefit. Becoming efficient must also produce a positive return on investment in terms of overall population health—the fundamental measure of performance in a medical marketplace.

Of course, economic analysis is not the only reason why health reform should be redirected as soon as possible. Political considerations are equally important in the context of public policy. Redirecting reform from reducing the number of uninsured Americans to reallocating wasted resources will not be worth the political price if the resulting improvement in population health is no greater than it would be under the ACA. If Democrats retain the power to protect the law by repairing it, its developers and defenders must be convinced that their long-run goals will be accomplished by going back to the drawing boards to build a world-class health system before expanding access. If Republicans win enough

Congressional seats to control the future of health reform, they will most likely need to develop "replacement" plans that address the production of health services. The standard Republican alternative to ObamaCare, a free market for health insurance accompanied by malpractice reform, does nothing to solve the fundamental problem of waste or create a world-class medical marketplace in the United States.

Finally, as shown in the previous chapter, waste harms patients, and not harming patients is the fundamental definition of professionalism in health care. Caregivers who control allocation of scarce medical resources should be dedicated to eliminating waste because it is the right thing—not the economic or political thing—to do. They should work to enlist purchasers and patients as their allies in a concentrated effort to become efficient by eliminating waste.

After 45 years in the medical sector, I believe that almost everyone who has worked in a health care organization will agree that providers and their business partners are extremely inefficient, that is, wasteful. (Even if they will not admit to being wasteful themselves, they will always agree that the provider down the street is.) When Mark Hagland and I were doing research for the first edition of this book in 2007, we searched the relevant literature and found several dozen articles that estimated the extent of waste in the medical sector of the US economy. Our review of these publications found estimates of overall waste ranging between one-fifth (20%) and one-third (33%) of national health care expenditures. Most estimates were near the high end of the range.

In 2012, the *Journal of the American Medical Association* published an article that reviewed an additional two dozen subsequently published reports on the topic.[1] This updated analysis found the range of waste from 21% to 41% of total spending on health care, with a midpoint of 34%. The authors, Berwick and Hackbarth, isolated and analyzed six specific categories of waste:

- Failures of care delivery
- Failures of care coordination
- Overtreatment
- Administrative complexity
- Pricing failures
- Fraud and abuse

Given widespread acceptance of the article's findings and absence of published evidence to the contrary, I feel fully justified in basing this book's analysis and recommendations on the assumption that 30% of all money spent on health care in the United States contributes nothing to the health of the population. Actually, it is a conservative estimate of waste in the American health care delivery system. It is also an embarrassing figure that ought to compel changes in the way we do business.

The economic value of the waste under this assumption is approximately $850 billion, which is 30% of the $2.8 trillion currently spent on medical goods and services in the United States. Ironically, the estimated costs of providing health insurance to all Americans ranged between $800 and $900 billion when the ACA was being drafted. The similarity of these estimates is purely coincidental, but it strongly supports my central premise in this book: Given the widespread inefficiencies in our medical marketplace, population health can be improved simply by reallocating wasted resources to the production of safe and appropriate health care for more Americans. However, the wasted resources must be reclaimed first by finding a different approach to health reform. The ACA does not take adequate steps in this necessary new direction.

Policy: One Size Does Not Fit All

Although health reform's first priority should be eliminating waste and reallocating the resources to productive use, legislative and regulatory changes to effectuate the shift must not fall into the trap of forcing all providers to redirect 30% of their

resources. One-size-fits-all reform will not eliminate inefficiency or facilitate much-needed innovation. Indeed, uniform
national standards for reform will make matters worse because
some medical enterprises waste a lot more than 30% of their
operating budgets and others considerably less.

Forcing already-efficient providers to do the same things as
inefficient ones creates the classic outcome of regression to the
mean: mediocrity. Reform is a mistake when it requires above-
average performers to take a step backward. Policy should
move all providers to economic excellence—100% efficiency—
without penalizing innovative organizations that have successfully captured and reallocated waste on their own initiative.
Because the path to efficiency varies widely across the medical
marketplace, policy makers must recognize the different prospects for efficiency on a case-by-case basis.

Policy makers must also be sure that reform's rewards and
penalties are directly linked to excellence in performance.
Compliance must be measured in terms of achieving efficient
outcomes, not in terms of adhering to tightly regulated production metrics, because there are many ways to cut waste. America's
exemplary health systems—the models for many provisions of
the ACA (Mayo, Geisinger, Kaiser-Permanente, Intermountain
Health, etc.)—have eliminated waste on their own by following
different paths. Of equal importance, reform laws have nothing to
do with their world-class successes. They should be rewarded for
continued success, even though they will achieve it in different
ways outside current confines of reform's uniform standards.

To the extent that reform compliance is enforced through
adverse consequences (e.g., sticks, not carrots), penalties should
be levied only on those organizations that continue operating
inefficiently. Reform should not reward organizations that do
everything required by the ACA but continue to waste billions
of dollars without improving the health of the populations they
serve. On the other hand, organizations that develop their own
ways to become efficient and expand access should benefit
from reform. Many organizations will succeed if reform rewards

them for accountable, goal-directed innovation in the context of their own circumstances and potential, rather than compliance with one-size-fits-all national standards.

Expecting successful and unsuccessful providers to do the same things in the same way has proven to be a counterproductive approach to reform. The federal government has imposed several uniform approaches to reform over the past 40 years, and not one of them has made health care more efficient overall. *Redirecting the government's reform role from dictating the means without specifying the ends to specifying the ends without dictating the means will be a major challenge, but I believe it is the most important step toward eliminating the paradox of American health care.*

What to Do with the Savings?

My analysis explicitly assumes that good reform policy would ultimately reallocate wasted resources to improving the health of our population. Internal transfers would maintain the medical sector at 17% of gross domestic product (GDP) under the no-growth scenario. This objective is the foundation of specific policy proposals in the final chapter. However, economic theory by itself does not guarantee achieving the 17% solution. For the same reasons that health care has lost its perennial claim to an ever-increasing share of the nation's output, health care has possibly lost its ability to retain what it has. Other sectors of the economy would love health care's loss to be their gain.

This point is not lost on many other economists and policy analysts, who agree that 30 cents or more of every dollar spent on health care in the United States is wasted. Several suggest that reform should aim to reduce overall health spending by 30%, and nearly all of them would agree with me that the ACA does not take meaningful steps in this direction. They argue—correctly, in my opinion—that we could produce today's quantity of health with only 12% of GDP. (A 30% cut from 17.2%, health spending's current share of GDP, is 12%.)

If we are happy with what we have, improvements in efficiency can produce it for a lot less money. Corporate purchasers of employee health insurance often take this position; they see a 30% cut in their benefit costs as money available for other purposes. The logic of simply cutting 30% from health care spending is also supported by international comparisons. A few dozen foreign countries with comparable economic systems have populations at least as healthy as ours; paradoxically, they only spend around 12% of their total output on health care.

I cannot disagree with the logic of those who argue the United States would not necessarily be hurt by an across-the-board 30% cut in health spending. Today's health care really could be produced for 12% of GDP if the delivery system were 100% efficient. However, I strongly disagree with the lack of vision in this approach to reform. Rather than accepting how much less we could spend to get what we have while watching 5% of GDP go to other uses, I prefer to focus on how good our national health could be if current resources were used productively.

Thus, reform's redirected goal should be to create the healthiest population that 17% of GDP can buy. The medical sector is, after all, a major source of national strength. From the perspective of social welfare, it is arguably better than most other sectors likely to capture resources from health care. From an economic perspective, health care businesses create economic strength in many desirable ways, both domestically and internationally. However, inefficiency is not the only issue as redirection of reform gives health care the chance to live up to its full potential. Effectiveness, the subject of the next chapter, is at least as important.

Note

1. D. M. Berwick and A. D. Hackbarth. Eliminating waste in US health care. *JAMA*, 2012;307(14):1513–1516.

Chapter 4

The Clinical Imperative: Effectiveness (Quality)

Introduction

Efficiency is not the only performance measure for which health care lags behind almost all other American industries. Providers of medical services also have a general and, sadly, merited reputation for being ineffective. To survive in highly competitive markets where the overall quality of products has become as important as the costs of producing them, leading companies in nonhealth sectors of the economy have been forced to become effective—to tell customers what to expect and to deliver as promised. The same disciplined improvement needs to be brought to the medical marketplace.

Effectiveness is not the same thing as efficiency. The common practice of using *efficiency* and *effectiveness* as synonyms is wrong and misleading. Businesses in a particular industry can be efficient and ineffective or inefficient and effective. You can have one without the other. For example, Japanese cars were sold at remarkably low prices when introduced to the American market in the 1960s because they were produced very efficiently. These imports quickly developed a reputation for poor performance and low quality. They were ineffective products. Japanese automakers sold a cheaper car in the United States but did not originally give consumers what was expected in an automobile. Cars from Japan sold poorly and became the metaphor for shoddy goods, even though they were relatively inexpensive.

We all know that the current situation is quite different. Japanese companies ultimately focused intense efforts on producing a car that would appeal to the American motorist. In less than two decades, they set and met standards that established their "foreign" cars as best buys in the American market for automobiles. ("Foreign" is in quotation marks because Japanese auto makers also became efficient by assembling many of their cars in the United States, thus avoiding high costs for transporting finished automobiles across the Pacific Ocean. Ironically, the consultants who taught them how to master efficiency and effectiveness were Americans—but that is another story.)

Effectiveness: Compliance with Specifications of Performance

The basic concept is simple. Effectiveness is a relative measure of compliance with objective specifications of expected performance. If a good or service does everything that it was designed to do, it is 100% effective (regardless of its cost of production or price). If it performs below specified expectations, it is correspondingly less effective. Take, for example, a robotic drug-dispensing system that is designed to fill 1,000 prescriptions every hour. If it correctly fills only 900 prescriptions per hour, the device is 90% effective because it is achieving only 90% of its promised performance.

Readers who do not remember studying effectiveness in Economics 101 will probably remember studying it in an introductory statistics course. Most statistics textbooks illustrate the concept with a problem set in which a random sample of a product (e.g., a light bulb) is selected off the assembly line, the items in the sample are tested, and the number of defective products in the sample is compared statistically with the number of defects allowed by the production specifications. An equation extrapolates the sample test results to the entire production run, incorporating the desired level of confidence in the results. The batch is accepted if the rate of defects is below a predetermined threshold defined as effectiveness in production. If the number of defects exceeds the threshold of statistical significance, the production process is reengineered to be effective. (Whether the defective batch is kept off the market is another issue.)

The basic statistical methods for judging actual performance against specified performance are generally categorized under the heading of process control techniques. Six Sigma, total quality management/continuous quality improvement, and Lean manufacturing are familiar examples of management methods that use process control techniques to improve effectiveness. The tools of process control are usually designed for the specific purpose of cutting waste and producing better products. They bridge the gap between efficiency and effectiveness, as demonstrated in several of the following chapters.

Neither Cost nor Value

In both consumer economics and production engineering, effectiveness is an important consideration at the interface between customers' expectations and producers' promises. Consumers and producers both want effective products. For example, if an automobile conforms with the manufacturer's published specifications—it really gets 32 miles per gallon and goes 100,000 miles without services other than periodic maintenance, as advertised—the car is a very effective product for the company that made it and for the customer who bought it. Neither the buyer nor the seller incurs any unexpected expenses or unpleasant surprises. Effective products clearly help create consumer satisfaction, product loyalty, and other valuable "blue sky" assets for sellers in any industry, including health care.

The automaker's cost of production is not included in the measurement of effectiveness. A car that meets all expectations could be produced efficiently or inefficiently. Effectiveness also is not determined by the purchase price. The financial deal struck between the dealer and the buyer does not have an impact on the car's mileage, service record, comfort, safety, or other performance measures. To prove the point, we have all probably bought both a lemon from a high-priced auto dealer with a gleaming showroom near an upscale mall and a completely satisfactory car from a guy in a plaid suit at a lot on the rundown side of town. Our experiences show that an expensive product does not necessarily meet expectations, and an inexpensive product can exceed them.

The subjective relationship between price and consumer satisfaction is *value*. It has nothing to do with effectiveness (or efficiency, for that matter). Value will be extremely important to the success of hospitals and medical groups in the new marketplace where purchasers are operating with fixed budgets. However, *health care delivery organizations must master efficiency and effectiveness before they can produce true value*. Real value cannot exist if products are overpriced or underperforming in a competitive marketplace. Value-based purchasers who have choices want to know what they can reasonably expect for their money.

Some health care providers get it backward, trying to sell value without first doing the hard work of defining effective services and producing them efficiently. This approach will be increasingly unsuccessful as the medical marketplace becomes even more competitive, for several reasons:

■ **Expanding scope of geographic market**: Providers have believed for years that all health care is local. Patients presumably shop close to home, even when they could save money or get better care by going to providers in another marketplace. There is no compelling reason to become efficient and effective if the services of other local providers are no less expensive or no better. However, recent changes in consumer behavior clearly indicate that patients will leave the home market when they are required to pay a significant portion of the bill. Medical travel, both domestic and international, has become common over the past decade and continues to grow. Many major employers even pay travel costs when their employees can obtain a better deal from a distant provider, and America's world-famous providers are building programs to attract patients from across the country. Providers everywhere must become efficient and effective because the medical marketplace is not local any more.

■ **Expanding scope of product market**: Until recently, the delivery of health care services was defined by a face-to-face encounter between a physician and a patient in a hospital or medical office. This effective monopoly, through providers' control over the time and place of caregiving, has come to an end. Patients now have direct access to fully qualified nonphysician practitioners in most states.[1] Nurse practitioners, certified registered nurse anesthetists, certified nurse midwives, clinical pharmacists, and advanced practice therapists deliver many services that were previously provided only by physicians. Research consistently shows that the quality of their care is at least as good within their defined scopes of practice and that consumers are extremely satisfied with the new caregivers.

Together, these two new forces are making medical care available in many new sites, especially commercial spaces like neighborhood retail centers and shopping malls. National pharmacy chains and urgent care centers are increasingly and successfully competing with hospitals and medical offices. Expanded hours and immediate appointments make these new delivery sites and caregivers popular with a growing number of patients. Mobile technologies are also expanding patients' options in time and space. Web-enabled devices provide many personalized health services at any time and any place, while telemedicine has continued to expand the scope of services that can be provided at the work site and in the home.[2] These alternatives to traditional care models are explored in more detail in the next chapter as essential tools for achieving efficiency and effectiveness.

■ **Expanding availability of consumer information**: Recent advances in the medical marketplace directly challenge a long-standing assumption that "health care is different" because consumers do not have information about their health and would not understand the information if they had it. Thanks to the accelerating proliferation of consumer information technologies (e.g., Internet, web, smart devices, apps), consumers can access a wealth of information about signs and symptoms, possible diagnoses, and treatment alternatives. Once they have a sense of the care they need, consumers can also identify providers ready to meet their needs. They can evaluate online reviews of the treatment options and the providers competing for their business. Some prices are already available, and more information about costs of care will become available with the growth of reference pricing. Failure to compete in the infosphere will increasingly mean failure to survive in the marketplace. For those who do compete, transparency and accountability will be prerequisites for success.

Why Effectiveness Is an Imperative

The effectiveness imperative for executives and trustees is to make sure that their health care delivery organizations do the right things in the right sequence. *To be effective, providers must specify the quality of the good or service they are going to produce.* In other words, the first step for any provider organization that aspires to be demonstrably effective—a critical success factor in competitive, accountable, and resource-limited industries—is to state objective criteria against which performance will be measured.

A precise set of performance criteria effectively becomes the road map for the production process; it specifies the destination and provides the mileposts to measure progress along the journey. Only then can resources be allocated and managed to meet the performance objectives. Specifications must be developed before production begins; effectiveness defined after production is completed is meaningless. Again, if you do not know where you are going, how will you know when you get there? More important, how will your customers know that you took them to the expected destination if you did not tell them what to expect?

Being graded in college is another useful analogy because hospitals and medical groups are starting to receive many grades. A grade should measure a student's effectiveness in meeting a course's objectives. As students, we resented professors who did not announce the criteria for grading before we took a test—especially when we put a lot of work into answers that seemed important to us but apparently not to the professor. On the other hand, we liked teachers with clear grading policies because we could do our work already knowing how it would be judged. Hospitals and medical groups can reap comparable benefits by announcing objective criteria for grading before their work is put to the test.

Beyond serving as a foundation for performance assessment and improvement, measures of effectiveness also define the long-run destination for a medical enterprise. They establish the level of performance that will be used to grade the organization's output of goods and services in the future. Therefore, an organization's directors and senior executives have a strategic responsibility to commit their organization to measurable effectiveness. They must be the champions for reallocating resources as necessary and holding everyone in the enterprise accountable to specified levels of performance. Conversely, if leaders with strategic responsibility do not issue a system-wide mandate for effectiveness, the action probably will not be taken by anyone else within the organization—giving a big advantage to competitors who do.

Once top leadership has adopted effectiveness as a strategic imperative for the entire enterprise, tactical managers must have the responsibility and authority to meet the measurable objectives of performance. Again, an analogy helps to illustrate the point. The strategic leaders in a health care delivery organization are like a visionary architect who creates the concept drawings that are entered in a competition for a building project. The provider's department managers are like the engineers and designers who prepare the blueprints and the workers who do the construction for the architect whose concept is selected. The final result is best when the strategists are responsible for defining and enforcing vision and the tacticians for organizing and executing performance. Top-level leaders must clearly communicate an orientation to effectiveness in the organizational vision that line managers are responsible for actualizing, but they must let the managers do the work.

Effectiveness and Quality in Health Care

Effectiveness in health care delivery can be assessed with several nonmonetary measures. (In economic analysis, money is not a valid measure of effectiveness. The cost of production in dollars is a measure of efficiency, not effectiveness.) Consumers might judge the effectiveness of providers on the basis of waiting time, personalization of service, or convenience of location. Providers might use accreditation, public designations (e.g., "top 100" status), or market share to judge their own effectiveness. Buyers and sellers do not necessarily use the same criteria to measure effectiveness, a point commonly made by automobile industry analysts and certainly relevant in health care.

Fortunately, quality of care is rapidly emerging as a common standard for measuring effectiveness in the medical marketplace. Quality is not the only criterion that consumers and providers might agree to use for measuring effectiveness, but I believe it is the one with the most appeal to all concerned—especially in a business that makes the difference between life and death and consumes one-sixth of our gross domestic product (GDP). Therefore, the analysis throughout this book assumes that quality should be the number one criterion to measure effectiveness in the American health care delivery system. (In the impish spirit of Michael Feldman, who tells *Whad'Ya Know* listeners to get their own radio show if they do not like the answers to his quiz questions, I suggest readers write their own book if they think something else is more important than quality in responding to the effectiveness imperative.)

Concepts like value and consumer satisfaction play important supporting roles, but quality must trump all other considerations when strategic choices need to be made in health care delivery organizations. Quality should not be compromised for potential gains in other dimensions of effectiveness. Seeking anything other than the highest possible quality is increasingly likely to backfire in the emerging medical marketplace. Last, and definitely not least, for reasons elaborated in the previous chapter, professionalism compels providers to defend quality as the number one criterion for gauging their work. Quality is the twenty-first-century embodiment of Hippocrates's enduring challenge to health professionals: "First, do no harm."

Quality: Consistent, Appropriate, and Safe Care

For quality to become a meaningful and preferred measure of effectiveness in health care, it must have a consistent definition. The concept as currently applied is too nebulous to be operationally useful as a foundation for redirecting health reform. The word *quality* undoubtedly appears in the mission statement of every provider organization in the country. Yet, we are all aware of enormous regional and local variations in the processes and outcomes of care.

The quality of medical care in America runs the gamut from excellent to abysmal. The same can be said about quality within many provider organizations. I have worked in hospitals that provided the best of care *and* the worst of care on any given day. If all the providers in the country consistently lay claim to producing "quality" health care, then the word as currently used is meaningless. It cannot be a differentiator when it encompasses everything across a broad spectrum of performance from bad to good at the same time and even within the same organization.

Quality needs qualifying adjectives to become meaningful. I believe the word must be preceded by *consistent, appropriate*, and *safe*. I expect smarter commentators will ultimately suggest even better adjectives, especially as data and analytics continue to improve, but the use of *quality* without meaningful adjectives should not be allowed in future discussions of health reform. We need a precise concept to refocus reform on precise actions and outcomes. (To this end, I suggest that a new acronym should be at the center of any effectiveness-oriented discussion of quality: CASC, for consistent, appropriate, and safe care.)

Consistent must be part of a uniform definition for the reason noted: Organizations that provide good and bad care are performing inconsistently, and the bad care is a big part of the 30% waste in our medical marketplace. Consistency means that consumers can expect the same quality of care every time, of course, but it does not tell them whether they will obtain the good or the bad on any given day. Hence, *appropriate* and *safe* must also be part of the definition of quality to ensure that the right care is provided in a way that does no harm. In the absence of these modifiers, a provider could receive high quality marks for low-quality care. For example, a hospital that provides error-free back surgery (e.g., no infections or other complications, no postoperative readmissions) 100% of the time is nevertheless providing bad care for any patients who were not appropriate candidates for the procedure.

The good news is that progressive delivery systems and professional associations are defining quality in ways that allow quality to be the valid (i.e., meaningful) and reliable (i.e., accurate) measure of effectiveness. The common denominator across these efforts is total commitment to consistent, measurable, science-based standards for evaluating the delivery of medical services at all stages of each patient's care. The measures being used may vary from institution to institution, but all institutions share a commitment to a formal process for providing every service consistently, appropriately, and safely. If an organization does not have a process for enforcing these criteria for a given service, the organization should not be providing the service.

Redirecting Reform: Performance Standards to Standard Performance

America's world-class health systems have crafted exemplary quality assurance processes in consideration of their unique, individual circumstances. Because of many differences between them (e.g., history, legal organization, business model, markets served, size), all have achieved excellence in different ways—reinforcing my conclusion that one-size-fits-all approaches to reform are neither necessary nor helpful. The common denominator of excellence across all these top-performing health systems is unyielding dedication to performance improvement, and there is more than one viable approach to incorporating performance improvement into every aspect of daily operations.

Consequently, as reform is redirected from expanding access to promoting efficiency and effectiveness, providers and their business partners need to be held strictly accountable for standardizing performance at the highest possible level all the time. This essential next step toward defining world-class excellence in health care is different from reform's current approach, one that imposes the same performance standards on all providers less than all the time.

For example, current reform laws regularly define quality compliance as meeting federal performance standards (i.e., quality indicators) 80% of the time, measured after the fact. Conversely, proven processes for standard performance (a distinction elaborated in the next chapter) are applied to every step in a production process while it happens. I believe the difference between 80% performance standards and 100% standard performance is reason enough to redirect the existing approach to health reform. Why? Because meeting an 80% performance standard allows as much as 20% of production not to meet expectations. By extension, paying for 100% of services billed by a provider that meets 80% performance standards is potentially paying for 20% of services that are deficient. That is waste—a big reason why we need a new and better approach to reform.

Either way, quality health care is becoming synonymous with *quantified* health care. Progressive providers have therefore been learning how to define quality numerically, not just verbally. Ironically, in a semantic twist, quality as the measure of effectiveness in health care must be defined quantitatively—not qualitatively. The structure and process descriptions of traditional accreditation mechanisms (e.g., "Our hospital has committees that meet weekly and review selected cases") are completely inadequate for the new task. Hospitals and medical groups must produce valid and reliable numbers to support prespecified measures of providing quality care for every service delivered, and they must make this information available to consumers. Without supportive and publicly available data, the quality measures in a typical mission statement or strategic plan will be meaningless.

An organization's leaders must respond to the effectiveness imperative with policies that impose data-driven processes at all stages of operations. Strategic plans must be updated as necessary to shift the enterprise's quality statement from rhetorically subjective (e.g., "We work as a team to provide quality care") to accountably objective (e.g., "We standardize performance according to best practices and undertake corrective action to prevent recurrence of any deviations from expectations"). As more provider organizations make this necessary shift, the definition of quality will evolve from a fuzzy philosophical concept to a meaningful operating reality.

Limitations of Historical Efforts

Quality has been a major concern since the 1960s, when Professor Avedis Donabedian established structure, process, and outcomes as the standard measures for grading and comparing health care delivery systems. Safety was added to the list of qualitative criteria during the 1990s. The Joint Commission for Accreditation of Healthcare Organizations (JCAHO, now known as the Joint Commission), other industry accrediting groups, and government regulatory agencies continually refined their methods for evaluating providers on the basis of these four criteria. Compliance with these organizations' published standards and regulations was deemed to be an adequate proxy for the quality of a provider's health services.

However, several well-publicized studies by the Institute of Medicine (IOM) and other independent organizations demonstrated that providers were not producing a consistently good product, even when fully accredited. Hundreds of thousands of avoidable deaths and injuries were directly attributed to flaws in delivery—care that obviously did harm. Decades of self-enforcement through accreditation have not ensured the production of truly effective health services. In response, groups of experts have promulgated several dozen quality indicators over the past decade and linked them to reimbursement with a reform policy called pay for performance (P4P). At first, meeting the standards was rewarded with a small bonus, but not meeting them can now result in slightly reduced reimbursement in some cases (I personally wonder why deficient care should be reimbursed at all, an issue already raised by Medicare's refusal to pay for "never events").

Pay for performance is not without serious flaws. Many of the quality indicators have been criticized for insensitivity to clinically significant differences in patients who are being treated for a given diagnosis. Again, 100% compliance with the standard for administering aspirin to 80% of all patients with heart attacks does not produce quality medical care for the patients who should not take aspirin—even though it does reward the provider financially. The conflicts will undoubtedly be resolved over time, but today's quality indicators do nothing to guide the operational changes that providers must make to survive in a no-growth medical marketplace. Bonus payments for performance are "a drop in the bucket" compared to total resources that providers will need to stay in business. And, as implied by my parenthetical comment at the end of the previous paragraph, the logical result of P4P is nonpayment for nonperformance. Effectiveness is all the more imperative under this scenario.

Effectiveness Comes from Within

Partisan gridlock will prevent governments from solving the quality problem in the foreseeable future. The deeply flawed implementation of the Affordable Care Act also raises serious questions about governments' abilities to manage health reform. Likewise, the health care industry as a collective entity will not produce timely solutions because of its internal divisions, intense competition, and related issues of antitrust law. The history of collective efforts to improve quality over the past 40 years clearly suggests that hospitals and medical groups will need to become effective on their own, one provider at a time.

Performance standards can enhance a provider's production processes when appropriately adjusted to reflect clinically significant differences in patients with the same general problem, but reform's proclivity to one-size-fits-all standards is counterproductive. Further, performance standards do not include useful information on how to reach them. Hospitals and medical groups need to develop and follow their own operational procedures that produce the desired results. Fortunately, health care providers can adopt and adapt production systems from other industries that have already overcome their own financial crises by becoming efficient and effective.

Understanding and applying this lesson is one of the most important contributions that a leader can make to a successful future for his or her organization. Setting and meeting objective, real-time measures of performance is the key to survival in the emerging medical marketplace where nobody is willing to pay more for what they get and everybody can go somewhere else for what they want. To paraphrase a statement often made about a treasured pastime, like fishing or golf, "Becoming an effective health care delivery organization is not a matter of life and death. It's more important than that."

Pursuing Efficiency and Effectiveness Together

Really astute readers have probably foreseen the possibility of an inconsistency in my analysis. I have made compelling arguments for efficiency and effectiveness, which might give the impression that I am now going to claim that hospitals must become as efficient *and* as effective as possible. This conclusion sounds good, but it is incompatible with a key point from the previous chapter: Only one variable can be maximized or minimized in a system with fixed resources (i.e., no growth). A combined goal of producing the highest possible quality of care at the lowest possible price simply "does not compute." (Accomplishing this goal for everyone, the hackneyed mantra of reform, is even more absurd under current economic and political circumstances.)

Therefore, health care's strategic decision makers must decide whether efficiency or effectiveness is the variable to be optimized by their organization. They must choose between being as efficient as possible for a fixed level of effectiveness or being as effective as possible for a fixed level of efficiency. Either option is feasible. However, for two compelling reasons, I advocate the first choice: minimizing cost or maximizing output (efficiency) for providing services that are as consistently good as they can be.

■ Effectiveness, defined as quality, should not be a variable in health care. First, it is an absolute obligation of the healing arts. Second, variations in quality will decrease an organization's competitiveness when consumers, who are being expected to spend more of their own money on health care, can easily compare the quality of competing providers. If consumers want to know what they can reasonably expect from a hospital or medical group, quality should be a constant (i.e., services meet specific quality criteria because they are produced according to standardized processes). Admittedly, studies have not yet demonstrated that data on quality significantly influence consumers' choice of providers, but the foundations for major impact have been laid. The number of data-rich resources for quality comparisons is proliferating, as is the number of patients who now "have skin in the game" with high-deductible health plans. Even a relatively low proportion of quality-informed consumers, say one-third for reasonable argument's sake, would be enough to justify fixing quality standards at the highest level if—as might reasonably be expected—these are the patients most likely to pay their bills. Allowing variations in quality seems therefore financially destructive in the new, information-rich medical marketplace.

■ Efficiency is the variable to operationalize once quality is established and assured. I have not forgotten that the main reason for updating this book is my conviction that providers must plan to live with the level of real (i.e., inflation-adjusted) revenues they are receiving now. Payers and consumers are certainly not willing or able to pay more money just to keep hospitals and doctors in business. Therefore, providers need to produce top-quality medical services—doing things right all the time—as efficiently as possible. Waste must be cut from operations because net revenues cannot be reliably increased. The difference between fixed revenues and declining costs is, at the bottom line, the only money that most providers can capture to make strategic investments in the personnel and technologies of twenty-first-century health care. It is also the only source of resources for expanding access in the foreseeable future, the 30% waste that can be captured and reallocated with a realistic redirection of health reform.

Hospitals and other provider organizations must find the most efficient way to provide consistently appropriate and safe health care. Quality (effectiveness) is the fixed factor in the production equation. Cost (efficiency) is the variable. Making this commitment will be a major challenge for most providers, but it is an imperative for all in today's medical marketplace.

Setting the Standard for Quality

Provider organizations need to shift their long-run thinking in order to survive, from complying with uniform performance standards 80% of the time to standardizing performance for being effective 100% of the time. The shift will require most providers to address serious shortcomings in their existing approaches to quality. They will need to develop and enforce standardized production processes in organizations where individual practitioners have been free to practice the art of medicine "their way" rather than adhere to an institutionally standardized science of acceptable practice.

The individualist tradition substantially explains quality and cost problems that are inadequately addressed by reimbursement-centered reform. Pay for performance is at best an indirect mechanism for building a better health care system, and the P4P thresholds are not much of a stretch from the traditional baseline. Providers can accomplish marginal improvement in compliance with quality indicators by making tactical changes. They are not compelled to make transformative strategic changes, such as redesigning production processes, changing the personnel assigned to a task, or even redesigning the product.

Hence, reform focused on reimbursement is a poor way to start building a world-class health care system. It is well-intentioned incrementalism, but it does not impose changes that get to the crux of the quality and cost problems that in turn cause America's access problem. Rather than struggling to meet the short-term requirements of a poorly crafted and inconsistently implemented law, providers need incentives to intervene first in the production of medical services. And they need to accomplish this clinical transformation on their own, sooner rather than later, because successful government-driven solutions are unlikely to occur under current political circumstances. Indeed, most providers I know are so bogged down in trying to comply with today's reform laws that they do not have time to work toward becoming efficient and effective so that more patients can ultimately be served for 17% of GDP. The opportunity costs of the current approach to reform are enormous, I am sad to say.

A Model for the Effectiveness Transformation

Transformation of the airline industry provides an excellent model for health care providers to follow. The effectiveness of commercial aviation was recognized as a serious problem in the last decades of the twentieth century. Fatalities occurred at an unacceptable rate, so the industry engaged external experts to help isolate the causes of preventable crashes. (Not surprisingly, the ineffectiveness of health care is often described in terms of two or three 747s crashing every day—a scary, unflattering analogy that should shame us into action.)

Careful studies showed that nearly all airline accidents were caused by human error, and fatal errors were frequently committed by pilots with the most hours of flight experience. Experts concluded that too much importance had been assigned to experience and not enough to the way pilots actually flew the planes. Airline crashes were almost completely eliminated when the carriers standardized flight procedures for all pilots. Simulators were used to ensure consistency in training and performance. A culture of safety was created, with special mechanisms created to reward—not penalize—reporting of errors. All critical incidents were investigated, and requirements for standard performance were updated as necessary to prevent errors from happening again.

Commercial air crashes were almost completely eliminated by the beginning of the twenty-first century, thanks to the development *and enforcement* of consistent performance criteria, uniform training, team development, human factors engineering, and standardization of equipment. Paying a little bit more to pilots who followed the rules was not part of the solution. All pilots were expected to perform according to the new, standardized procedures or find another line of work. (Ironically, airlines discovered that their best pilots were those hired with the Federal Aviation Administration minimum number of flight hours. The less-experienced pilots were generally better at learning to fly safely "by the book." Many of the most experienced pilots had trouble conforming to standards because they had spent so many hours developing their own style of flying.)

Effectiveness for Health Care: Doing It Right

Because lives are on the line in health care and air travel, commercial aviation's compelling lesson for health care is to pursue the goal of absolute effectiveness, that is, operating without avoidable errors or unexpected variations. Hospitals and medical groups must adopt the proven tools of management engineering, performance improvement, and business model transformation to ensure that every service is provided the right way, all the time. Once correct techniques have consistently become standard operating procedures (SOPs), providers can then devote their efforts to optimizing efficiency. I know that many readers will think the goal of eliminating avoidable errors is unreachable in health care, so I now turn to chapters that explain viable approaches to efficiency and effectiveness.

If skeptics remain, I ask them a simple question: To save money, would you be willing to get your health care from a provider that publicly admits its care is not always as good as it could be? (For example, "We comply with performance standards 80% of the time.") I do not think you would be any more willing to patronize this provider than you would be to fly on an airline that advertises getting you, not just your luggage, to your destination most of the time. Hence, I propose a simple slogan for providers that accept the imperatives of efficiency and effectiveness: *Delivering health care right all the time, as inexpensively as possible.* This statement should be in every provider's strategic plan. Now, let us see how to deliver as promised, at prices consumers are willing and able to pay.

Notes

1. For extensive analysis of the foundations of this development, see Jeffrey C. Bauer. *Not What the Doctor Ordered.* New York: McGraw-Hill, 1998.
2. For an introduction to this technological advance, see Jeffrey C. Bauer and Marc A. Ringel. *Telemedicine and the Reinvention of Health Care: The Seventh Revolution in Medicine.* New York: McGraw-Hill, 1999.

Chapter 5

Tools for Efficiency and Effectiveness

Introduction

The corresponding chapter in the first edition of this book was built around case studies. Mark Hagland and I were eager to tell the success stories of a few dozen exemplary provider organizations that were leading the revolution to bring efficiency and effectiveness to the medical marketplace. Readers' responses over the years expressed considerable appreciation for the information. Therefore, I begin this chapter by explaining several reasons why I am not including case studies in the revised edition.

■ First, case studies about performance improvement (PI) programs have become ubiquitous in the intervening years. The organizations we featured six years ago have expanded their efforts and continued to share their experiences through many articles, books, and conference presentations. Several other health systems and their business partners have joined the list of progressive organizations that not only recognized the need for strategic change but also did something meaningful about it and willingly

shared what they learned. Consequently, there is no need
for me to add to the extensive body of existing resources
that describe what has been done. Readers who are interested in case studies can consult any number of online
and print resources made available by professional associations and government agencies (e.g., American Hospital
Association [AHA], Health Information Management
Systems Society [HIMSS], Healthcare Financial
Management Association [HFMA], Agency for Healthcare
Research and Quality [AHRQ]); health care business
publications (e.g., *Healthcare Informatics*, *HealthLeaders*,
Modern Healthcare); and book publishers (e.g., CRC Press,
Health Administration Press, Jossey-Bass).

■ Second, the business of health care is changing so fast
that information in any format is not necessarily current
for long. Case studies that defined the state of the art only
a year or two ago are likely to be outdated; they should
only be used as templates for future action after verifica-
tion of their strategic relevance. I have stayed in touch
with several of the organizations featured in the first edition of this book, and they have continued to innovate on
the leading edge. Their actions were "ahead of the curve"
when Mark Hagland and I wrote about them six years
ago, but their original solutions have evolved significantly
because of new developments in medical science, technology, consumer demand, and even health reform.

■ Third, case studies are organization specific, and organizations are unique. No two have the same human and
capital resources for solving problems, and problems that
look alike on the surface can be quite different across
different organizations. I therefore hesitate to highlight
approaches that worked somewhere in recognition of
the common tendency to assume they should be repli-
cated elsewhere. For example, a program that improved
quality or reduced costs in an academic medical center in

midtown Manhattan is unlikely to be directly transferrable to a critical access hospital in the Rocky Mountain west. Unfortunately, case studies of successful PI programs are used to create one-size-fits-all regulations and demonstration programs under our current reform laws—a practice that hinders much-needed innovation in a highly diverse, fast-changing marketplace like health care.

Although case studies have limitations when applied across different organizations and over time, they are excellent resources for teaching innovation and problem solving. Consequently, I encourage leaders to seek case studies not as timeless examples of specific ways to make health care efficient and effective, but rather as inspiration for creating world-class health care delivery systems through strategic actions (i.e., reallocating resources). Transformation of this magnitude requires specific tools, so I have "reallocated" this chapter's content from a compendium of case studies to a description of the tools needed to produce medical care efficiently and effectively for the foreseeable future. Historical case studies may not show how to do it now, but they show that it can be done by progressive organizations acting on their own in a timely manner. On the other hand, waiting for federal guidance can be fatal.

Least Common Denominator: Information Technology and Digital Transformation

Health care has a remarkably low level of automation for a personal services industry. For comparison, try to imagine a bank without an interactive network of automated teller machines (ATMs) and online financial services that allow its customers to conduct their financial business at any time of day without going to a bank. An airline without online reservations, ticketing, and check-in is just as hard to picture in today's marketplace. A major retailer without an online store is equally unimaginable; shopping over the Internet has become completely natural. Automation has been a win-win for sellers and buyers. Any bank, airline, or national retailer that tried to force all its customers back into a line to conduct a transaction with a clerk would soon be out of business. It is clearly time for the medical sector to join the rest of the economy.

Providers have no choice but to automate in order to meet the imperatives of efficiency and effectiveness. Labor costs, especially the value of caregivers' time, will continue rising because of limited supply. Hiring more labor is obviously a losing proposition in a marketplace where labor is becoming more expensive and real revenues have quit rising. Consequently, productivity of the existing workforce must be improved, which compels providers to increase investment in nonlabor inputs. Hiring more workers, even if they were available, would not solve the problems of cost and quality because these workers would need more and better information to do the job right all the time. In terms of economic theory, health care is at the point at which the marginal returns to technology are generally higher than the marginal returns to labor. Making the required trade-offs is the price to be paid for survival in the new medical marketplace.

Somewhere around seventh grade, we all learned about the lowest or least common denominator (LCD) as an essential key to solving problems. A multifactorial equation cannot be solved until every factor rests on the same common numeric base. By analogy, a common denominator is necessary for solving cost and quality problems in health care because processes for becoming efficient and effective are data driven. A staggering volume of information from across the enterprise is required to find the least-expensive way to provide health care of expected quality with standard performance processes. All these data must be tied together with an LCD before meaningful progress can be made. Health information technology (HIT) is the only tool that can do the job.

The data-processing power required to produce medical services efficiently and effectively transcends the capabilities of paper-based data systems, yet health care is still largely stuck on a paper trail that does not lead to a better delivery system or a healthier nation. Health care simply cannot reach its full potential until it is supported by a state-of-the-art infrastructure of information technology (IT). Real reform requires digital transformation—adopting IT tools to automate work that was previously done by people processing paper and relying on their memories to connect information.

As "the HIT Futurist," I preached digital transformation and automation in the lead article of every issue of HIMSS' *Journal of Healthcare Information Management* from 2001 to 2013. HIT is the essential foundation of PI through standardized processes, and my firm commitment to it has not changed. This is not to say that HIT has not changed over the same years. It has changed considerably because of the Healthcare Information Technology for Economic and Clinical Health (HITECH) program, a key section of the American Recovery and Reinvestment Act (ARRA) of 2009.

HITECH authorized somewhere between $20 and $30 billion, depending on how you interpret the law, to reimburse "qualified providers" for new investments in electronic health records (EHRs), interconnected systems, and training programs needed to become "meaningful users" of "certified" commercial systems. (Some lawmakers tried hard, but unsuccessfully, to use HITECH to impose a government EHR on civilian providers.) Although $20 or $30 billion may sound like a lot of money, it is considerably less than the amount needed to adopt modern IT across the entire health care delivery system. When HITECH was being drafted, estimates for full conversion (including mine) ranged between $100 and $120 billion. Congressional leaders in both parties were seriously seeking ways to find the money until politics (in particular, a senator's switch from Republican to Democrat) diverted potential funding to other uses as the price paid to pass ARRA.

HITECH's supporters argue that the law has pushed digital transformation in a good direction, but I am among many who disagree. The $20 to $30 billion final appropriation was completely insufficient to support the necessary conversion, and five years have been spent pursuing a scaled-back goal driven more by politics than efficiency and effectiveness. Like the Affordable Care Act (ACA), HITECH has not been implemented as enacted. Constant, unpredictable change in regulations and deadlines during the implementation period has created a lot of cynicism, even hostility, toward adoption of EHRs. Many physicians believe that automation has decreased their productivity and have some believable evidence to back up their claim.

Because of prolonged implementation, more and more chief financial officers are concluding that participation in HITECH is causing their hospitals to lose money. However, from my economist's perspective as a believer in creative destruction, HITECH's most negative consequence is that it stifles innovation. (Creative destruction is Joseph Schumpeter's principle, presented in *Capitalism, Socialism, and Democracy* (1942), that technology-based innovation creates economic progress by replacing established production techniques that have outlived their usefulness.) To qualify for HITECH's financial "incentives," providers have been forced to adopt EHRs and related systems that adhere to a uniform set of federal standards, even though providers have widely different needs. Many of the regulations seem to be created by bureaucrats who do not understand the complexities of day-to-day patient care, another factor that prevents desirable HIT innovation.

Participating providers have spent more time trying to comply with ambiguous, rigid-but-changing government guidelines than innovating to improve efficiency and effectiveness. Providers are bogged down in a regulatory process that moves slowly compared to the rapid evolution of technologies and applications. In contrast, America's world-class health systems mastered the process of digital transformation before HITECH was even created. They did it because it was the right professional thing to do, and they did it many different ways. These differences are reflected in the recommendations in the final chapter of this book.

Note: Although Americans use HIT in writings and discussions on the subject, Europeans use HICT (health information and communications technology) to highlight the link between information *and communications* technology in state-of-the-art health care applications. I use HIT as the acronym in this book because it is written for an American audience, but I would adopt HICT if I did not think an explanation would be required with each usage. Communications technology is a big part of the big picture. Information systems will not solve many problems if they cannot communicate with each other. Connectivity and interactivity are every bit as important as hardware and software. HITECH deserves credit for recognizing the importance of this point, even though the *C* for communications is missing from its title.

Data and Analytics

Data and analytics deserve treatment separate from health information technology in a chapter on the tools needed to build the best possible delivery system for 17% of the gross domestic product (GDP). Information technology and digital transformation will generate an unprecedented and increasing volume of data (i.e., raw numbers), but these numbers do not automatically turn themselves into useful information (i.e., organized data). Technology for collecting information and systems for using it are not the same thing. Different tools are needed to ensure that the data and information are themselves efficient and effective.[1]

Machines beat humans hands down when it comes to making fast and accurate calculations, but only humans can decide if the calculations are worth making. Consequently, the first and most important tool in data analysis is a human expert with a keen eye for the quality of the numbers collected, stored, retrieved, and analyzed by the IT. This process for data quality control has not yet been automated, and I doubt that it ever will be because it requires careful attention to the validity (i.e., meaningfulness) and reliability (i.e., accuracy) of the numbers before they are entered into an IT system.

Two related attributes of data deserve leaderships' attention.

■ First, the timeliness of data (i.e., whether they are up to date). Old good data are important for historical analysis, but current good data are essential for making good strategic decisions. Leaders should also demand efficiency in their organizations' information systems. Health care's databases typically include a plethora of useless information—numbers of no real value, even if they are valid, reliable, and carefully managed. It illustrates the old farmer wisdom that anything not worth doing is not worth doing well.

I have never seen an estimate of the money wasted on outdated and useless data, but health care IT experts seem to agree when I suggest that the sum is substantial. HITECH's acceptance of existing EHRs wastes a lot of money to the extent they include unnecessary information. A redirected health reform plan should allocate resources to rebuilding the medical record from scratch, including only data that are needed for efficient and effective health care. Reform can do better than using twenty-first-century technologies to automate a medical record designed for twentieth-century medical practice. We need EHRs that reflect and reinforce current concepts of care and cure.

■ Second, the quality of data. "Garbage in, garbage out" (GIGO) was common knowledge when computers became available for health services research in the 1960s. (Trust me; I was there.) GIGO has been forgotten or willfully ignored over the years, but it is as important as ever. Leaders must therefore demand that only good data are analyzed by their information technologies. Sadly, many of the computations used to create provisions of the ACA were performed on bad or outdated data, which explains some discrepancies between high expectations when the law was passed in 2010 and disappointing realities of implementation in the following years.

Big data became the "next big thing" after HITECH and ACA were passed. The concept offers considerable promise to aid efficiency and effectiveness, but is not a panacea for several reasons that begin with bad data. The most sophisticated analysis of invalid or unreliable numbers can only make matters worse. Also, big data excels at identifying correlations but does not have the power to differentiate between useful and meaningless relationships. Good research methodology dictates that hypotheses be formed before data are analyzed because random relationships are remarkably common. Unfortunately, big data allow analysts to charge ahead without exercising forethought. This practice can easily lead to false conclusions and bad decisions, especially when used by people who know nothing about the numbers they are mining.

e- and m-Health Technologies

Reaping the full benefits of digital transformation requires more than automating health records (assuming valid and reliable data). Two relatively recent developments, e-health and m-health (mobile health), provide additional tools for becoming efficient and effective. Both are evolving at a rapid pace and proving to be popular with caregivers and patients. Indeed, nurses and physicians are already becoming creative with their use of e- and m-health technologies—often deploying them without official approval because these technologies facilitate their work. This do-it-yourself movement already has its own moniker, BYOD (bring your own device). Provider organizations ignore the potential contributions of these technologies at their peril.

The e- prefix is borrowed from the first letter of *electronic* and has been used for several years to characterize corresponding technological advancement in a variety of domains (e.g., e-mail, e-commerce). Although e-health is used to encompass several dimensions of health care, the e-concepts provide essential foundations for automation and PI processes. One of the most impressive examples is using websites as hubs for exchange of information between all the parties involved in each individual's health, such as consumer portals that improve outcomes by informing consumers about their care.

More recently, progressive providers have begun using m-health technologies. The m- is for *mobile* and refers to the rapidly growing realm of smartphones and other conveniently portable, wireless, app-enabled devices that enhance the multiple interfaces between providers, payers, patients, and information. I definitely see mobile technologies becoming deeply embedded in health care delivery when I look in my crystal ball as a health futurist. Indeed, m-health devices and integrated systems are positioned to provide the heretofore-missing links between inpatient and outpatient care, caregivers and patients, and dispersed sources of information about each individual patient.

An old reform goal, patient engagement, is taking on a whole new meaning with the adoption of e- and m-health technologies. Interactive communication offers many opportunities to overcome roadblocks that create waste in health care. The capability to share information across personalized, user-friendly interfaces is particularly promising because it overcomes shortcomings of one-size-fits-all solutions in a population of highly diverse patients. Evolution of e-health will also move providers close to a paperless environment, eliminating much waste in the process. (I intentionally stop short of using *paperless* as a part of the definition of e-health. Paper will not completely disappear any time soon.)

The smartphone alone offers amazing potential to improve efficiency and effectiveness in health care. Linked to a rapidly expanding array of web-enabled devices, handheld communication devices may be the LCD for solving some of health care's most persistent problems. Imagine how a smartphone integrated with a personal website could improve almost every dimension of a patient's interactions with the health care delivery system, eventually replacing the massive information exchanges currently being constructed. If smartphones can acceptably manage other complicated dimensions of our lives, why not our health care?

Information technology continues to generate even more tools for bringing efficiency and effectiveness to health care, including social networks and intelligent information resources. Organizational survival without a state-of-the-art online presence using these tools is unimaginable in today's competitive marketplace, especially as transparency and accountability become more important factors in consumer choice. However, the functions of online services are evolving at a remarkable rate that requires constant attention to updating them with e-health and m-health technologies. Success also requires constant attention to integrating of all these tools across the enterprise.

Telemedicine (Telehealth)

Health care was defined throughout the twentieth century by face-to-face, hands-on visits between a physician and a patient. State medical practice acts and reimbursement regulations effectively prevented other approaches to health care. Almost all the data used to study health care since the 1960s were collected in hospitals or medical offices and then made available to researchers and policy analysts through government agencies or third-party insurance companies. This traditional organization of medical care delivery has impeded progress as new technologies create opportunities for qualified caregivers and patients to interact not only from different locations but also at different times. This is the twenty-first-century realm of telemedicine (telehealth).

Telemedicine replaces traditional medical services with new approaches that can be at least as effective as hands-on care, and it can be more efficient (i.e., less expensive) when properly integrated into care delivery. Some organizations have adopted money-saving telemedicine systems but tried to maintain face-to-face pricing. However, successful adoption requires passing some of the savings along to the customer in today's cost-conscious medical marketplace.

One of the best-known examples of telemedicine is tele-radiology. It is made possible by well-established systems of interactive digital technologies that allow a diagnostic image to be acquired from patients in one location and interpreted by distant radiologists (often in another state or even in a foreign country). It allows an image to be interpreted by a far-away specialist with skills that local radiologists do not possess, or it allows a radiologist in another site to make a diagnosis when no local radiologist is available.

Information and communications technologies also allow remote critical care specialists to manage patients in several intensive care units at one time, a highly efficient practice that has saved money when an expensive, on-site specialist would have been underutilized at any single location. Telemedicine also extends professional care into patient's homes, work-places, or other locations via affordable equipment that can capture diagnostic-quality information from the patient. Video links can establish face-to-face communications when neces-sary. With remarkable improvements in photo and video capa-bilities, smartphones are rapidly becoming key components of these virtual systems for delivering care.

Unfortunately, state medical practice acts and reimbursement regulations are still mostly stuck in the twentieth century when it comes to recognizing telemedicine's contributions to efficiency and effectiveness. The redirection of reform needs to nurture provider-payer collaboration to eliminate economic barriers and other disincentives in the many instances when telemedicine is a cost-effective alternative to face-to-face care. This goal needs to be specifically incorporated into the redirected approach to reform because political forces have generally protected the status quo as telemedicine has developed into a mature, proven substitute for traditional care. However, as noted, providers should agree to pass along some of the savings as their contribution to progress.

Having proven its value in delivering many services of acceptable and defined quality at lower costs, telemedicine should be a part of any provider's strategic planning process—automatically considered as a tool for modernizing any existing service or developing a new one. Telemedicine should also be evaluated as an alternative to building more physical space, such as using virtual consultations to reduce the need for exam rooms. Today's telemedicine also knows no geographic boundaries; it is for providers anywhere. Its predominant identification with rural health is an unfortunate vestige of twentieth-century health politics. We must move beyond considering it to be a "second-best" solution for people who live in remote areas with small populations and few caregivers. Virtual care is a proven tool for providing efficient and effective health care in every geographic setting.

Input Substitution

One of the most powerful concepts in the economics tool kit is input substitution. Anyone who has taken Economics 101 should remember the theoretical elegance of replacing one input with another when the new input does the job at least as well for less money. Efficiency and effectiveness depend on it, as illustrated by telemedicine's capacity to lower overall costs of care by reducing the need for exam rooms and radiologists—not to mention savings in transportation costs and carbon footprint (by eliminating patients' trips to hospitals and radiologists' travel between facilities), reduced risk of disease transmission in waiting rooms, and easy access to imaging specialists.

Digital transformation and telemedicine both illustrate productive trade-offs between two of the three traditional factors of production: labor and capital. (The other traditional factor is land; information is now generally identified as a fourth factor.) However, some of the most beneficial trade-offs occur within a single factor of production, such as replacing one type of labor with another. Labor substitution occurs in the medical marketplace, but not nearly as fast as it must if we are to quit wasting money when acceptable services could be provided by an equally qualified, less-expensive health professional.

Hundreds of publications validate qualified nonphysician practitioners' contributions to efficiency and effectiveness. Indeed, our world-class health systems are leaders in replacing physicians with nurse practitioners, clinical nurse specialists, certified nurse midwives, clinical pharmacists, and therapists with doctoral degrees. I have written extensively about using nurse practitioners and certified registered nurse anesthetists as substitutes for physicians. Although many doctors and professional associations have challenged my conclusion, none has ever produced a single peer-reviewed, research-based article to contradict it.[2]

Given the well-documented benefits of labor-labor substitution within defined scopes of practice, redirecting reform will require a serious commitment to making it happen. Many special interests, especially medical specialty associations, have fought hard to prevent competition from nonphysicians.

(In many instances, they devote equal effort to defending their "turf" from physicians in other medical specialties.) Reform leaders must be willing and able to challenge defenders of the status quo—the uniquely American way of delivering health care that wastes 30 cents on the dollar and receives a comparatively poor return in population health. To win these battles, leaders must show that the issue is not who has the most years of training, but who is the least-expensive professional with demonstrated competency to provide clinical interventions of defined, acceptable quality.

Success in physician versus nonphysician battles will require compromise on both sides. Physicians must admit that other health professionals can learn to do many things at least as well without going to medical school, and the non-physicians who have gained these comparable skills must understand that they cannot use reform to be paid physicians' traditional fees in a marketplace that has quit growing. In fact, today's economic realities are much more likely to drive down the higher incomes than to raise the lower ones. The key to success is building clinical teams focused on efficient and effective care, where qualified teammates trust each other to provide a service for which they have demonstrated competency and to refer it to someone more qualified when necessary. Given the unprecedented complexity of health care today, no single provider can do it all alone. (I am pleased to acknowledge the many progressive physicians who accept qualified nonphysician practitioners as teammates who can provide services independently.)

Input substitution works as well in practice as in theory when "all other things are equal." Economists make this ceteris paribus assumption because other factors often get in the way of rational economic behavior and optimal outcomes. Monopolies and political power, for example, are forces that have consistently impeded scientifically defensible, technologically possible input substitution in health care delivery. We should not, therefore, be surprised that waste is so abundant in the medical marketplace. The 30% of spending that contributes nothing to our population's health is income for many individuals and organizations. This problem must be addressed head-on if the potential of American health care is to be fully realized through redirection of reform.

To extend the sports analogy of using input substitution to create diverse teams for victories in cost and quality, the playing field also needs to be leveled. Providers and their business partners must find it in their economic self-interest to become efficient and effective. Recent studies have shown that the current payment system tends to do exactly the opposite. Under our fee-for-service (i.e., volume-based) reimbursement system, PI programs that successfully eliminate wasteful care result in a loss of the revenue a provider would have received from delivering it. Doing the right thing can be financially detrimental, much more often than not. Redirecting reform will require restructuring economic incentives so that providers cannot make more money by delivering care that does not improve individual and population health—even if the unnecessary services are flawlessly provided.

The Performance Improvement Imperative

Building a solid foundation for world-class health care across the United States will absolutely compel providers to use another powerful tool—a formal performance improvement (PI) program that affects the delivery of every service across the enterprise. Regrettably, PI is not a requirement of the ACA. The relatively small number of providers participating in demonstration projects might use a PI tool in pursuit of their goals, but it is optional. Although everyone laments the ACA's failure to bend down the cost curve, I am more disturbed that the law does not bend up the quality curve with a sensible and viable requirement for PI. This concern is the basis for a key policy prescription (recommendation 2) in Chapter 6.

Mark Hagland and I devoted a whole chapter and more than a dozen case studies to PI in the 2008 edition of this book because the tool was so seldom used in health care at the time. My discussion can be much briefer in 2014 because PI has gained attention and acceptance in the intervening years. Indeed, most provider organizations have already implemented at least one PI project, but one is not enough. Now is the time to move to across-the-board adoption of PI for all providers and their business partners.

Performance improvement must become the guiding principle of efforts to redirect reform because waste cannot be recaptured and reallocated until this shift is made. Replacing the ACA's insurance mandate with a PI mandate as soon as possible is the only feasible way I can see to find the resources for subsequent reforms in a marketplace that has quit growing. It will not be easy, but it is necessary if our long-term goal really is efficient and effective health care for all Americans. Getting there will take several steps, beginning with universal PI.

Performance improvement is a general rubric that encompasses several different approaches to the same goal: reducing cost and improving quality. Mark Hagland and I explored five well-known means to this end in the previous edition, expecting to identify the best one while gathering information from several dozen providers that had made institutional commitments to PI. We discovered that each of the different PI systems had produced impressive gains in more than one organization, and none had failed.

We therefore concluded that the key to success was carefully implementing and continually operating a PI program. (We did find a few exemplary providers that simultaneously used several different tools at the beginning of their PI activities, but all ultimately adopted a single approach for consistency across the enterprise.) The commitment to getting the job done, not the specific tool used, was what mattered most. It became a core component of each organization's culture.

My experience since then has reinforced this conclusion. Consequently, the rest of this chapter presents an updated overview of information that leaders can use to initiate PI, if they have not already done so, in the context of what works and does not work in their organization.

Experience with PI in a wide range of industries, including health care, provides several good reasons for selecting a proven methodology—as opposed to starting from scratch—for managing the necessary improvements in organizational performance.

- Tools with a track record (i.e., those supported by how-to books that have sold well and articles linking them to successes in a variety of industries) provide a common understanding of the process that will be followed across the enterprise. They are, in effect, the same page from which everyone should be reading.
- Because proven PI tools have been tested and refined in many organizational environments, they are already tailored to the demands of making systemic changes in dynamic marketplaces. They will provide much-needed confidence in the process because stakeholders will know they are using a PI tool that already worked well in comparable settings.
- The established tools define appropriate investments in staffing, training, education, and IT. Because the leading PI systems have evolved over many years—none of them being really new—they help prevent underinvestment in managerial and clinical areas that are critical to success.
- Because they are data driven, these established tools generally provide useful performance benchmarks for getting started. Organizations that use objective data as required by the processes are much more likely to make appropriate adjustments that will lead to success. They will become learning organizations through PI if they have not already achieved this important organizational characteristic.

Negative knowledge—knowing what not to do—will help providers avoid problems that have plagued narrowly focused "quality improvement" projects in health care organizations for many years. Most programs that failed in the past did not incorporate the comprehensive mechanisms built into today's PI and clinical transformation tools.

- Unsuccessful programs did not enforce unswerving commitment and direct involvement from the top of the organization. The failures of PI "lite" projects can often be attributed to lack of time and money invested by the board, medical staff leaders, and executive managers.
- Unsuccessful programs tended to focus narrowly on specific "mechanical" problems, such as streamlining the admitting process or reducing waiting times for diagnostic tests. They did not address the fundamental interconnectedness of all the processes that are involved in the care of each patient.
- Failed PI efforts were not explicitly linked to an organization's vision, mission, or strategic business goals. Consequently, they almost never became core values that permeated the enterprise and defined the corporate culture across all disciplines. They did not define "this is how we do things here" in any special way that also defined the organization.
- Narrow, single-service quality improvement programs almost always fell short in integrating with IT and providing needed data. They did not generate the extensive information needed to coordinate ongoing changes for accomplishing quantified goals.
- Unsuccessful programs often resulted in little more than disappointments and, even worse, layoffs. Employees became quickly disenchanted with PI programs because single-function efforts tended to do more harm than good in the final analysis. They were true examples of the uninspiring French adage, "The more things change, the more they stay the same."

With this background to guide the search, executive summaries of the most common PI methodologies are presented now for leaders who are responsible for deciding what needs to be done, to ensure efficiency and effectiveness throughout their organizations, but not knowing how to do it. Line managers with responsibility for selecting, implementing, and maintaining a specific PI program will have no difficulty finding excellent resources for getting the job done once the decision to do it is made. Here are viable options that have been successfully used in leading health systems:

■ **Lean management** is one of the two most common PI tools in health care today. Lean is not an acronym that should be capitalized, but rather a reference to the physical state of having no excess fat on the bones. It evolved from the *Toyota Production System* (TPS), which focuses an enterprise on eliminating identifiable waste (e.g., producing too many goods or services, creating excessive inventories, wasting time or effort, making worthless movements, etc.). TPS accomplishes the task with a sharp focus on consistency (*kaizen*)—something clearly missing in the delivery of our health services. The system also focuses effort on team approaches to problem solving that draw on human skills (*jidoka*) and long-run approaches to decision making. Its powerful principles were popularized (in a good sense of the term) in the United States under different names, most notably total quality management/continuous quality improvement (TQM/CQI).

One of America's most successful and dramatic shifts from waste to efficiency and effectiveness, at Virginia Mason Medical Center in Seattle, was driven by TPS.[3] However, the same core principles with descriptive names in English are more often applied now in Lean management programs. Lean operationalizes familiar terms like key performance indicators, just-in-time performance, root cause analysis, error proofing, work flow analysis, and work process control.[4]

Like TPS, Lean provides a comprehensive system for standardizing and streamlining activities to eliminate waste through management engineering across the enterprise and over time. It directly links to strategic goals, helps define an organization's core values, and enforces a sharp focus on producing value for consumers. All these features need to be added to health reform as it is redirected from access to efficiency (value) and effectiveness (quality); these features are not explicitly promoted in the ACA.

- ■ **Six Sigma** is the other PI tool most commonly used in health care. *Sigma* is a statistical term that represents a standard deviation from the midpoint of a normal distribution, where ±1 sigma encompasses a bit more than 68% of all values. Six Sigma is way, way out on the tail of a distribution and represents 99.99966% of the values. The corresponding error rates are approximately 300,000 per million operations at ±1 sigma and 3 per million at ±6 sigma. Obviously, a hospital operating at six sigma is way, way better than one operating at one sigma. Six Sigma is a desirable goal for reforming the delivery of health care; the experiences of America's best health systems show it is an achievable one.

The Six Sigma PI system, originally developed by the Motorola Corporation, is built on a concept called DMAIC (define, measure, analyze, improve, control). It begins by defining a problem in practical, measurable terms and follows a graphic process to eliminate defects at all stages of the production process. Improvements are identified with powerful statistical techniques that identify critical-to-quality (CTQ) requirements and are managed by formally trained experts with certifications representing demonstrated levels of competence, from green belts to master black belts.

The process actively involves quality councils of people involved in production and operates under the guidance of project leaders known as champions. Like the Lean tool, Six Sigma is intensively focused on providing quality from the customer's perspective; the voice of the customer (VOC) is a central tenet. It is also iterative, meaning quality control is a constant process that permeates production at all times. It is based on the demonstrated principle that quality can always be improved.[5]

■ **Hybrid approaches** can work just as well if one of the other tools does not provide the impetus an organization needs to start getting the job done. I generally favor using a single methodology for eliminating waste because Lean and Six Sigma are each supported by excellent training materials and support systems, but a few American health systems have achieved world-class success with a combination of key concepts from two or more PI tools.[6] Their impressive transformations give credibility to a hybrid approach.

In addition to borrowing components of Lean and Six Sigma, hybrid approaches draw frequently on the Plan-Do-Check-Act (PDCA) system and a closely related process known as Balanced Scorecard (BSC). Both involve regularly repeated analyses to examine and guide convergence toward specific goals, specifically avoiding the very real problems of "paralysis by analysis" or "the perfect as the enemy of the good" that cause a quest for perfection to produce nothing at all.

A constant, enterprise-wide focus on moving in the desired direction is common in other industries and can fit well in health care. A provider organization should not be dissuaded from using a hybrid approach if its managers and consultants have the skills to achieve desired results with a formalized process that is not Lean or Six Sigma. Moving forward right now with a PI tool that works is far more important than waiting for the perfect tool.

Expert Consensus: Tools for Changing the Future

Experts in the various PI methodologies have their biases, but they tend to agree on one important point. For business organizations in any industry to apply PI successfully, the enterprise needs to do so strategically. Leaders must be committed to making changes and reallocating resources for the explicit purpose of creating a specific, desired future that is different from the future likely to occur if nothing changes. The requisite changes include creating new corporate cultures and new ways of thinking. Hiring enough management engineers and other qualified efficiency experts is usually the biggest challenge. (The outside experts do not necessarily need to have experience in health care; indeed, some of the best solutions have been produced by teams of health professionals working with PI experts who come from other industries.) Consultants can get the job started, but I believe that an internal department of full-time employees is ultimately necessary.

The proven PI tools are meant to create big changes across the enterprise, not to "fix" small problems within a broader context of business as usual. They allow employees to work together in highly complex environments, unquestionably today's situation in health care. With the science and technology of medical care changing faster than ever before, producers of medical services need PI tools to be able to adapt to constantly changing circumstances. Consequently, PI tools require ongoing, enterprise-wide education that teaches everyone how to recognize and solve problems collaboratively.

When workers are well trained in the chosen PI process, they are empowered to call a halt when they see a problem that could lead to a production error. They are also empowered—indeed, expected—to make changes that will prevent the problem from occurring again, in contrast to health care's long-standing practice of finding "workarounds" instead. Executives who champion the implementation of PI in their organizations must therefore select a methodology that educates and empowers personnel to do the right things, all the time. When this philosophy becomes part of the corporate culture, the enterprise is positioned to meet the imperatives for efficiency and effectiveness in all that it does. That is real health reform.

Skeptics often raise a concern that PI tools were designed for the automobile industry, something very different from health care. (My graduate school mentor, Kenneth Boulding, conversely claimed that hospitals were just like automobile repair shops, only cleaner.) When Mark Hagland and I conducted interviews with PI experts from automotive firms, we found several uniform characteristics that are totally relevant for today's health care providers: (1) Corporate leaders and managers have created a shared, sustainable philosophy around their quality mission and have set operational goals to meet customer needs and expectations. (2) The core philosophy is founded on a culture of quality and excellence that constantly strives for improvement. (3) Every aspect of production processes is continually questioned by a team of employees who are given a democratic voice in promoting change.

Is there a reason why health care delivery should not work like this? Had one posed this question to hospital executives only a few years ago, the response would likely have been that delivering care to patients in hospitals is nothing like producing cars and other consumer goods. Fortunately, a growing number of executives and clinical leaders of progressive health systems across the United States have decided that better health care can be produced along these lines. In fact, they have been aggressively studying PI techniques and applying them to health care delivery with remarkable success.

Progressive executives and clinical leaders have been pushing health care to become like other industries—to become customer responsive because purchasers, payers, and consumers are demanding greater value—while the media publish stories on dangerous gaps in quality and embarrassing statistics about waste. Outsiders are raising awareness of quality problems and forcing providers to respond in public. Performance improvement is thus an imperative because the medical economy has quit growing and health professionals are ethically obligated to do better. The growing number of successes in cost reduction and quality improvement puts real pressure on the many hospitals that have not yet responded. Arguing "health care is different" is no longer defensible. It has fallen far short of its potential and needs to catch up, sooner rather than later.

Notes

1. For extensive discussion of these points and their relevance to health care, see my book: Jeffrey C. Bauer, *Statistical Analysis for Decision-Makers in Health Care*. 2nd edition. Boca Raton, FL: Taylor & Francis Group/CRC Press, 2009.
2. See J. C. Bauer. Nurse practitioners as an underutilized resource for health reform: Evidence-based demonstrations of cost-effectiveness. *Journal of the American Academy of Nurse Practitioners* 22(2010):228–231.
3. A useful overview of Virginia Mason's turnaround is presented in Charles Kenney's *Transforming Health Care* (Boca Raton, FL: CRC Press, 2011). I reference it frequently in my speeches on the future of health care.
4. Details for implementing the process are found in Mark Graban, *Lean Hospitals*. Boca Raton, FL: CRC Press, 2012.
5. For a thorough introduction to the Six Sigma approach to PI, see Charles T. Carroll, *Six Sigma for Powerful Improvement: A Green Belt DMAIC Training System*. Boca Raton, FL: CRC Press, 2013.
6. An impressive example of do-it-yourself PI is the Baylor Health System. Complete details of its customized approach to PI are presented in David J. Ballard, editor, *Achieving STEEEP Health Care*. Boca Raton, FL: CRC Press, 2014.

Chapter 6

Redirecting Reform: Strategic Recommendations

Introduction

Repair, repeal, or replace? That is the trillion-dollar question about the Affordable Care Act (ACA) as I write this chapter in mid-2014. However, none of the three proposed answers gets to the core of the problem. Repairing the law might overcome fatal flaws created in the frantic haste to get it passed, but the crux of the law would still be focused on reducing the number of uninsured Americans. Repealing it is a waste of time as long as the president is a Democrat—a sure thing until at least January 2017—and something must be done before then. Replacing the ACA could potentially bring us closer to addressing the fundamental problem of American health care, but "replacers" have identified neither the problem they would solve nor their solutions for it. They seldom get beyond declarations that the United States already has the best health system in the world, implying there is no major problem with the system we have.

But, there is a monstrous problem, an "800-pound gorilla" that politicians are incapable of tackling. It is waste, the more than 30 cents of every medical care dollar that do nothing good (and often something bad) for the health of individuals and the population. Therefore, I propose that the answer to what to do about ObamaCare is redirecting reform to harness the wasted resources and then reallocating them to expanded access once the system is reliably efficient and effective.

We need to *redirect reform to build a good system first,* one worth extending to all Americans as soon as possible. Repairing, repealing, or replacing the ACA still leaves us with an inefficient and ineffective system that, as a rule, charges unnecessarily high prices for services of uneven quality with unacceptable commitment to value and consumer satisfaction. We can start by following the example of the exceptions that prove the rule—our world-class delivery systems that have achieved excellence on their own initiative and in different ways, long before the ACA was created.

Review of Reasons to Redirect Reform

The case for redirecting reform is based on several conclusions drawn in previous chapters. Moving in a different direction, rather than making minor or major adjustments to the general thrust of the ACA, is necessary because of the following:

▪ The medical marketplace is currently in a state of utter chaos, with the ACA at the center of the maelstrom. The hastily passed, poorly implemented law is not taking health care in any discernible or desirable direction. It does not provide a road map to a better health system, even in the unlikely event that it ultimately reduces the number of uninsured Americans. The current political situation—partisan, gridlocked, petty—is not capable of producing a national consensus on how to set things right. Further, the ACA's one-size-fits-all framework thwarts essential innovation in a diverse marketplace with many good possibilities.

■ The medical economy has quit growing. Because public- and private-sector purchasers who pay the bills for health care are neither willing nor able to spend more on health care each year, providers and their business partners need to learn how to survive on 17% of the gross domestic product (GDP). Raising prices or boosting volume are no longer the keys to providers' survival. The only realistic solution is to put top priority on building a health care delivery system that does not waste resources. Because government is not up to the task, private providers and their business partners must take responsibility, with unprecedented transparency and full accountability.

■ The magnitude of waste in the health economy is shameful from both economic and professional perspectives. A growing body of published studies suggests that somewhere between 21% and 47% of all money spent on health care does not contribute to the overall health of patients as a whole. Our medical expenditures do not pay off in health of the population. The United States spends a whole lot more on health care than all other developed countries, yet the health of its population is near the bottom of the same list. (I have conservatively estimated our waste at 30% of total health spending for the analysis in this book.)

■ Ample evidence shows that the delivery of medical services can be accomplished efficiently and effectively. Nothing about the provision of health care in the United States dooms us to squander 30 cents of every health dollar on duplicated efforts, unnecessary goods and services, sloppy work, flawed records, poor communications, inconvenient and insensitive service, unproven or discredited interventions, dysfunctional billing, and so on. A small but growing number of American health systems have used state-of-the-art information/communications systems and performance improvement tools to provide safe, appropriate, and consistent care (the world's best) as inexpensively as possible. Any provider organization that deserves to stay in business has an obligation to use these tools to do the right thing—a twenty-first-century interpretation of the health professional's primary obligation to do no harm.

Four key assumptions also lie behind my analysis and policy recommendations. Although they are not syllogisms in the classic sense, I believe the following assumptions logically lead to the same conclusion: Health reform needs to be pointed in a different direction, toward building an efficient and effective health system, before it returns to the highly politicized goal of access. My assumptions are the following:

■ The broken American health care delivery system must be fixed; protecting the existing American model of health care will only make matters worse.
■ Economic growth cannot be expected to provide resources for fixing the health system; other sectors will claim any increases in GDP.
■ The ACA does not fix the system; mandating insurance to pay for a broken system is likely to create more problems than it solves.
■ The political dysfunction in Washington will likely continue for at least several more years; we must look elsewhere for leadership to build a good system.

Policy Recommendation 1: Limit the American Health Sector to 17% of GDP

Now is the time to act decisively on the national consensus that perpetual growth in medical spending is unsustainable.

It must stop somewhere—not only because of its poor rate of return in population health but also because it diverts resources from other essential sectors of the economy. The opportunity costs of health care's rampant growth have been less money for education, scientific research, civil infrastructure, and other foundations of a successful economic system. Putting a limit on medical spending is a key to overall long-term economic recovery.

Given the serious cost and quality problems that accumulated while health care grew from 4.5% of GDP to a high of 17.6% over the past 50 years, the "bottom-line" issue for public policy is determining an appropriate share of GDP to allocate to medical expenditures. Economics does not offer analytic tools for providing an objective solution, but I propose 17% as a logical limit. It is only slightly lower than the amount being currently spent on health care (17.2%), and analysis of current trends suggests we are likely to hit a 17% share about the time that this recommendation could be translated into national policy. Finally, maintaining 17% would not require cutting back resources from any of health care's special interest groups. Taking something away from the leading players would surely launch a bitter confrontation that would only make matters worse. It would be a battle not worth fighting, a no-win situation.

On the other hand, I have enough faith in today's leaders of the key special interest groups to believe they would agree to support a fixed limit as a preferred alternative to future battles over health spending in general and ACA reimbursement in particular. After all, health care's share of GDP could fall far below 17% under plausible economic and political scenarios. Medicare and Medicaid spending might plummet in coming years if not pegged to a bipartisan policy goal of stabilizing the size of the medical marketplace. If the ACA survives in anything close to its current form, it also includes dramatic long-term cuts in spending that would likely take health care below 17%.

Agreeing to protect the health sector's current relative share of national output would shift attention to doing the best we can with an amount we can afford rather than fighting for more—a battle that health care's special interests will find harder to win as others learn how much is wasted in the medical marketplace. Further, as already shown, a budget constraint is an essential precondition for efficiency and effectiveness. Today's waste was made possible by the blank checks that purchasers and payers sent to providers for so many years. Letting providers and their business partners know that they really will not be getting disproportionately more money will rivet their attention on performance improvement to reallocate wasted resources for better outcomes—a lesson quickly learned by other industries that quit growing. Performance improvement would be an explicit imperative under the 17% solution; it is only an indirect possibility under the ACA.

Another strong argument in favor of national economic policy to stabilize the medical sector comes from the other countries that spend 12% or less of their GDP on health care. Many American liberals want health reform to replicate foreign financing models, such as Canada's single-payer system or Great Britain's National Health Service, but government-managed systems are not the common denominator of health systems in the countries that produce healthier populations for a smaller share of national product. Most European countries have private insurance companies and private health systems, not completely socialized medicine. Deliberate steps toward even more privatization are now part of health reforms across Europe and in Canada. Moving the U.S. toward single-payer (i.e., government) reimbursement would actually be contrary to current health policies in countries that many liberals cite as models for American health reform.

Rather than government-owned health insurance and delivery systems, the common denominator in other comparable countries is national policy setting the total amount that can be spent on health care, but giving local authorities and private vendors considerable power to decide how the fixed budgets will be allocated. Our policy wonks should therefore be studying how countries with a roughly comparable mix of public and private providers (e.g., Germany, Holland, Belgium) have managed to produce healthier populations under government-established limits on total health spending. They will discover that consumers in these countries are quite satisfied with their health care; global budgets do not produce poor service.

I am far from the first person to propose a fixed target for the health sector's share of national economic output. Several other medical economists and policy analysts have evaluated the same economic data I have presented in previous chapters and concluded that the United States should cut health care back to 12% of GDP.[1] Targeting 12% is perfectly defensible. The European Union is the same size as the United States, and its members are the very same countries that collectively spend around 12% of national output on health care and have healthier populations than we do in the United States.

Why, then, do I propose redirecting health reform to freeze the American medical sector at 17% of GDP? The suggestion itself is perhaps paradoxical in consideration of the point made in the previous paragraph, but here are two reasons to take it seriously:

■ First, I personally favor extending good health care to all Americans, and I do not believe we could accomplish this objective at 12%. The argument in favor of cutting back says that our medical care system can do what it is doing right now for a lot less money, which is true. However, I would rather do more—expanding coverage as the next step in health reform after building an efficient and effective health care delivery system. (Previous sections of this book explain my belief that increasing access to a flawed system is not sound social or economic policy. I am committed to a long-run goal of providing good, basic care for all Americans—an outcome that is very unlikely to be reached via the ACA.)

■ Second, I proudly feel a commitment to American exceptionalism in health care. As the world's richest country, we should aspire to have the world's best health system. Our successful effort to eliminate waste would produce delivery system models that the rest of the world could adopt, just as other countries get the benefit of our international leadership in medical research and technology. The United States already subsidizes health care around the world by investing far more than anyone else in developments that improve quality and reduce costs, a "burden" that I am proud to bear. Ironically, our world-class delivery systems already export their clinical expertise to other countries. I look forward to the day when other countries will also want to adopt our health system model as well. (The European systems obtain a better bang for their buck, but they are far from 100% efficient and effective. We Americans could teach them a thing or two once we master the task of providing health care right, all the time, and as inexpensively as possible.)

Official authority to fix medical expenditures at 17% of GDP must rest with the federal government, but the necessary legislation should be developed in close collaboration with key stakeholders from the private sector. To begin, a bipartisan group of elected officials should convene a working group of leaders from provider organizations, health professional associations (including nurses, pharmacists, and other skilled practitioners), employers, insurers, and consumers for the specific purpose of drafting legislation to peg health spending at 17% of GDP. All participants should agree that the task is unprecedented, one requiring fresh thinking. They should look to European countries for models of how to accomplish it. They should also be constantly reminded of the Confucian wisdom that began this book: "Surely we will end up where we are headed if we do not change direction." We have got to change direction, and imposing a budget constraint is the best first step.

Am I being an idealist in making this recommendation? Absolutely. But, I am also being a realist in the analysis that leads to the recommendation. Staying the current course, including the ACA, will waste even more money and almost certainly fail to provide good, affordable health care to all Americans in the coming years. We can do better by finding a different and better way to get to the same long-run destination. Instead of continuing one more indirect approach to bending the cost curve under the guise of making care affordable, let us all agree to stop spending more and get on with giving providers the freedom to become efficient and effective, along with an unambiguous quid pro quo—no more money will be available to subsidize inefficiency and ineffectiveness.[2]

Policy Recommendation 2: Require Performance Improvement for Federal Reimbursement

Limiting medical expenditures to 17% of GDP will be just one more waste of time and money if reform is not simultaneously redirected to ensure efficient and effective health care. Federal and state governments have a long history of trying to cut costs and improve quality through reforms, but their track record is decidedly not good. Waste has grown over the past 50 years in spite of government's best efforts (i.e., complex rules and regulations) to reform health care. There is no reason to believe the ACA will reduce cost or increase quality any better than previous reforms. Indeed, given the incredible haste with which the law was finally passed, it could reasonably be expected to create an unprecedented number of problems. Haste, after all, makes waste.

Like previous reforms, ObamaCare relies extensively on practice standards to measure compliance with its goals. If a provider does not meet practice standards published by the Center for Medicare and Medicaid Services (i.e., fails to exceed a threshold number that defines minimally acceptable performance), the provider's reimbursement is reduced. The cumulative penalty for noncompliance can be as much as a 2% reduction in Medicare payments under current rules. Some analysts argue that the reduction in reimbursement is too small to improve performance, but I believe the amount of the penalty is a red herring in the broader debate on reform. The real issue is the numeric value of the threshold, which is currently 80% in most federal performance standards applied to health care providers. As noted in previous discussion, a provider can fail to perform acceptably 20% of the time and still meet an 80% performance standard. Is that reform? No, that is waste.

Simply raising the compliance threshold might seem like a good solution, but it is not appropriate in the delivery of health services. Patients do not all have the same needs, a fact that raises serious questions about using practice standards as a measure of quality in health care. For example, a current practice standard defines acceptable performance as giving aspirin to 80% of all heart attack patients within one hour of arrival at a hospital's emergency department. This is good medical practice for most patients, but some people should not get any aspirin at all. A hospital that gives aspirin to 80% of its heart attack patients meets the federal practice standard, even if some patients among the 80% should never take aspirin.

A good approach—one uniformly used by organizations that have eliminated waste, including America's world-class health systems—requires all caregivers to follow a standard practice (as opposed to meeting a practice standard), such as promptly evaluating whether an anticoagulant should be administered and, if so, which one (aspirin being one of several possibilities) is appropriate for each patient who comes to the hospital with signs and symptoms that might indicate a heart attack. A properly formulated, consistently applied standard practice is the key to ensuring that every patient receives the right care all the time, which is not necessarily the same care that other patients should receive. (Remember, developing a system that delivers the right care all the time is my number one goal for health care reform.) And, how does a provider make sure its caregivers are adhering to standard practices? That is the function of performance improvement programs, like Lean, Six Sigma, or a customized hybrid.

Consequently, reform's regulatory approach needs to be redirected from applying uniform practice standards across all providers to requiring every provider to use a performance improvement program that guides the delivery of all care and ensures corrective action to prevent any errors from being repeated. To make this shift happen, the new policy must be directly linked to a change in federal reimbursement. As a condition for receiving Medicare and Medicaid payment, providers should be required to prove they are consistently using a properly designed, institution-specific performance improvement program to do things right all the time, as inexpensively as possible. At least half of a typical provider's revenue comes from government programs, so this change in federal reimbursement policy would be enough to get a provider's attention and redirect performance in the desired direction. Most health insurance companies would quickly adopt the new federal policy; I do not see the need to legislate a separate policy change for private payers.

Nota bene: I am absolutely *not* proposing that the federal government develop a one-size-fits-all performance improvement program and impose it on all providers. I would actively oppose such action. Rather, the government's role in redirecting reform should be requiring each provider to prove it has developed and is consistently following its own standard practices and using its own performance improvement program. (For hospitals that are part of a larger health system, performance improvement programs designed by the system should be acceptable.) The role of Congress, in close collaboration with the special interest groups that must be involved in redirecting reform, is to craft legislation that liberates providers from counterproductive rules and regulations and, in exchange, holds providers responsible for doing better. Waste in the medical marketplace will continue until this transformation is accomplished.

Extensive regulatory relief is a fair and necessary quid pro quo to offer providers in exchange for requiring them to define their practice standards, identify unexplained deviations from expected performance, and prevent these deviations from happening again. Eliminating counterproductive regulations will be an essential step to keep providers in business during the transition. (I originally put *expensive* in front of *counterproductive* in the preceding sentence and then decided it was redundant. Compliance with federal regulations is expensive; it goes without saying.) I expect that tens of billions of dollars in annual costs would be saved in the process of eliminating the counterproductive regulations that divert health care executives from the critical task of reinventing the way health care is delivered.

With the likely end of growth in medical spending, providers simply will not have sufficient resources to comply with existing regulations *and* meet a requirement to develop their own performance improvement programs. Expecting health systems to do both at the same time would lead to massive financial failure on the supply side of the medical marketplace, with serious secondary consequences for the national economy. We need to keep the system relatively stable while undertaking the third recommendation for redirecting reform: developing a national consensus on expanding access to all Americans.

Before explaining the third and final recommendation, I must address the anticipated objections of policy analysts who will be appalled at the thought of reducing federal control over health care providers while giving them more authority and responsibility for the quality of services they provide. My recommendation is admittedly not a perfect solution, but we do not have the luxury of allowing the perfect to be the enemy of the good. Some providers will honestly try to improve performance and fail in the process, while others will cheat (e.g., intentionally misrepresent compliance) or find other ways to game the system.

However, I believe the vast majority of health care's executives and clinical leaders are honest, competent professionals who will embrace the opportunity to focus on performance improvement without the costly diversion of complex regulations written by bureaucrats who know little or nothing about providing health care. (Trust me; I have worked with all of them.) Free of regulatory compliance headaches, nearly all managers and caregivers will innovate and elevate the overall performance of American health care. Successes can be expected to greatly outnumber the failures.

However, the strongest argument in favor of redirecting reform might be that the traditional approach—new regulations piled on old regulations—has never made health care more efficient and effective. As Einstein noted, insanity is doing the same old thing over and over again and expecting different results. As Winston Churchill observed, you can count on Americans to do the right thing—after they have tried everything else. We are at that point; we finally need to look beyond creating even more one-size-fits-all regulations.

To be clear, I am not proposing a carte blanche that would allow health care's leaders to do whatever they want. The expectations of redirected reform will be extremely demanding and clearly stated. Failure to perform successfully will be costly for the provider—not for the taxpayer, as is currently the case because demonstrable performance improvement will be an absolute requirement for federal reimbursement. Another desirable trade-off would be reallocating money spent on regulatory compliance to identification and prosecution of health professionals who cheat the system. We could surely eliminate a lot of waste by increasing the risks of getting caught at fraudulent activity.

Policy Recommendation 3: Develop a National Consensus on a Good Health Care System

Having studied the medical marketplace and numerous efforts to reform it for almost 50 years, I have reached a conclusion that leads to this final recommendation: Our periodic efforts to reform health care are ultimately doomed to fail because Americans have never developed a shared view of the health care system that a majority would support, politically and economically. As I put it in the title of the last chapter of *Not What the Doctor Ordered*, "How will we know when we get there if we don't know where we are going?"[3] The final destination has never been clear, but that has not stopped health reformers from charging ahead.

Some are focused on lowering the costs of care. Others have wanted to improve quality or to move toward universal access. No matter what their primary goal, reforms' architects have created elaborate regulatory structures on the assumption that government action was needed to counteract health care's market failures. Then, the laws they created were continually changed by amendments. Two were ultimately repealed; one was never even passed by Congress (the Health Security Act of 1994, known at the time as HillaryCare). No major health reform since the Social Security Amendments of 1965, creating Medicare and Medicaid, has survived as enacted for long. Indeed, the ACA's problematic evolution is to be expected. Its creators spent almost no time trying to learn or apply the lessons of history; they were doomed to repeat the failures of previous reforms.

The reform cycle is predictable. Congress tends to draft a new reform law about every 10 years to solve a current economic problem—usually because the previous decade's reform did not stop "skyrocketing" costs as promised. However, lawmakers have never taken the time to develop a comprehensive strategic plan for the health care delivery system as part of a push for reform. Elected officials and their policy advisers have consequently been patching up a twentieth-century system that is showing its age, not using new tools to build a sensible, coherent system for the twenty-first century. Unless we actually enjoy doing the same thing over and over and getting the same undesirable outcome, Americans need to define the characteristics of the health delivery system they would like to have, *given what they are willing to spend*. It is the right thing to do and now the right time to do it.

I have concluded that a world-class health system in the United States should not consume more than 17% of GDP (Policy Recommendation 1) and that performance improvement tools should be mandated to make the system efficient and effective (Policy Recommendation 2) under any future scenario. I am confident that the vast majority of Americans will agree in general with both conclusions; I would not have taken the time to write this book if I felt the public would reject them. (I am an economist, not a masochist.) However, I am not so sure that my ideas for reinventing American health care would necessarily be the foundation for a consensus, and a consensus is what we need if we are going to build the world's best health system.

I was tempted to present my own blueprint for building a world-class medical care delivery system in this book, but that is not its purpose. For the record, I am strongly in favor of private-sector solutions created by multistakeholder partnerships that are publicly accountable for using an enterprise-wide performance improvement system to ensure all care is provided correctly, as inexpensively as possible. In exchange for a national policy commitment to hold health spending at 17% of GDP—possibly a gift to the industry because, without a commitment to hold the line, current trends are leading toward a share below 17%—providers and their business partners must be at risk to fail financially if they do not become efficient and effective and reallocate wasted resources to providing more care for the same money.

I am not philosophically opposed to a public solution that could be reasonably expected to achieve the same result. I still believe some functions must be performed by government agencies. However, my many years of firsthand experience with government health care makes me extremely doubtful that a successful public solution could be created or implemented under current political circumstances. Scientific and technological advances in health care also proceed much faster than public agencies and other regulatory bodies. A government-driven solution is almost certain to be obsolete by the time it is implemented.

We need courageous, selfless, forward-looking leaders in both political parties and other key communities—business, demographic (young and old, rich and poor, Anglo and not, etc.), and faith (including nonbelievers)—to organize an open-minded, national discussion about the health system we would like to have, plus the changes and compromises we are willing to make to build the system. The dialogue should be structured to define key features of a desired health care system, within the no-growth constraint. The convening leaders should not rush the process, but they should set a specific timetable and hold to it.

To get the ball rolling, I propose limiting the national dialogue to two years. A consortium of public and private organizations will be needed to provide funding for the process. (This would be a nice gift for the 1% to give back to the country, with no strings attached.) The process should not be overseen by government agencies. Political leaders must be involved, but the process itself must not be political. In addition, a few loud opponents must not be allowed to stifle discussion with inflammatory references to "death squads" and the like. They can make their point and then respectfully listen to everyone else or withdraw from the process.

Also to get the ball rolling, I propose an initial list of topics that *must* be discussed in the national forum to design a new health system. The leaders who facilitate the discussion and the institutions that underwrite it should definitely add to the list, but they should at least seek consensus answers to the following questions:

- **Individual right to health care**: Should health care be a right in the United States, like free K–12 public education? If so, how much health care is guaranteed? What is the appropriate balance between primary care and specialty care for individuals and for the population? Should the United States purposefully follow the lead of some other countries (e.g., Brazil) and intentionally operate a two-tier system with free public providers and private-pay, for-profit providers? How much free care should private health systems be required to provide?
- **Individual responsibilities for personal health**: Should patients receive ongoing treatment if they do not comply with caregivers' advice and prescriptions? How much time and money should be spent treating patients who do

not take care of themselves when properly told what to do and given the resources to do it? What health behaviors should cause a person to be denied care at public expense? Should deleterious products and behaviors be taxed specifically to subsidize care?

■ **Trade-offs** (yes, rationing): Stipulating that we Americans do not have the money to do everything that medical care is capable of doing, what are the basic guidelines for prioritizing care? Should patients be required to pay the difference when they want a good or service that costs more than the cost-effective treatment? Are Americans willing to accept medical professionals' recommendations for making wise choices?[4]

■ **Informed consent**: Assuming that Americans will continue to be required to pay an increasing portion of their individual insurance premiums and costs of care, what are desirable levels of patient involvement in making decisions about the care they receive? How can patients be adequately educated to understand and evaluate potential risks and benefits of treatment options? Should patients be required to participate in decision making for some types of care?

■ **End-of-life care**: Should preventing death be the absolute goal of all medical treatment? What is an individual patient's obligation to accept the possibility of death when physicians conclude additional treatment would be futile? Should health insurance be required to pay for futile care? Should family members be allowed to overrule a competent patient's decision to terminate treatment? How should caregivers and delivery systems inform patients about alternatives to care? Under what circumstances should discussion of end-of-life alternatives be required? When should patients have the right to choose to end their lives?

■ **Professional liability**: Is a bad outcome of care an acceptable ground for filing a malpractice claim in the absence of negligent practice? Should no-fault compensation for pain and suffering be made in cases of appropriate care resulting in bad outcomes? How can professionally adopted standard practices be used to eliminate unjustified malpractice suits? How should provider organizations enforce their caregivers' compliance with standard practices? (The answers to these questions should guide malpractice reform. However, the best solution to our malpractice reform is performance improvement programs that guide the delivery of consistent, appropriate, and safe care all the time. Let's put malpractice lawyers out of business by eliminating bad care, period.)

▪ **Access to care**: How far should patients be required to travel to get care at an efficient and effective facility? Should the health system subsidize rural hospitals that do not have the volume of services to support state-of-the-art care? Or, should the system subsidize transporting patients to the closest facility that is large enough to do health care right all the time, as inexpensively as possible? Should patients have insured access to physicians when equally qualified nonphysician practitioners are available at lower cost?

Again, this is a preliminary list of questions for a national dialogue to forge consensus on principles for restructuring the American health care delivery system. Quibbles about my sample questions must not be allowed to divert attention from the critical need for a truly democratic process. And, do not forget that I proposed these questions to get the ball rolling. I expect others to improve the list—and discussion participants to identify important issues that we experts overlooked.

A rural hospital closure back in 1989 offers a good model for developing efficient and effective alternatives when a local health system cannot always provide top-quality services as inexpensively as possible. The state health department summarily shut down the acute care hospital in St. John, Kansas (pop. 1,400) because the facility did not meet minimum requirements for licensure. Local leaders realized their community could not afford to operate a full-service hospital, but the state health department required all hospitals—small or large—to meet the same requirements. Under sponsorship of the Kansas Health Foundation, I facilitated a task force of innovative health professionals and 18 local citizens who selected options from a menu of desired health services and their associated costs. The members of the task force designed a "right-size" facility with a relatively short, carefully selected set of inpatient services that could be provided excellently and affordably.

The new St. John Primary Care Hospital was then remodeled and staffed solely to take care of hospitalized noncritical patients and to provide appropriate outpatient services. It developed a detailed clinical affiliation agreement with St. Francis Hospital, 95 miles away in Wichita, to accept patients needing higher levels of care, such as surgery requiring general anesthesia or cancer treatment requiring expensive technology. A state-of-the-art emergency medical services (EMS) system was simultaneously designed to stabilize critical patients in St. John and transport them via ambulance to St. Francis Hospital—alleviating need for a full-service emergency room that the small town could not afford.

St. John Primary Care Hospital immediately became the prototype for a federal program to save rural hospitals all across the country by giving rural residents local access to an integrated, full-service health system that provides top-quality services as close to home as economically possible. Not surprisingly, the resulting federal structure, now called the Critical Access Hospitals program, needs significant revision to incorporate changes in technology and medical economics over the 25 years since the first primary care hospital was created in St. John. The point not to be lost in this case study is that citizens were given the power to design a local health system they would use *and* could afford. Prices were on the menu before the order was placed.

If the next round of health reform has any chance at success, it must be built on a sense of where Americans as a group want to go with health care. It will almost surely fail if dictated by lawmakers, bureaucrats, and other "experts"; this is a lesson of history. I will be the first to admit that a sincere effort to build a consensus for reform might also fail. Our country may already be too polarized to solve its problems, but ultimately doing the right thing is part of American exceptionalism. When it works, it is done democratically—which requires knowing the will of the people before government takes action.

Conclusion

Departing from initial premises that no identifiable entity is controlling health care's destiny in the United States and that nobody knows for sure where things are headed—sure signs of chaos—I have come full circle to conclude that we must try to develop a national consensus of what we want from our medical marketplace, within the confines of what we are willing and able to spend. Like all previous reform laws, current and future efforts will fail until we have a clear blueprint for building a system that produces a healthy population at an expected and acceptable cost. The critical question of the moment is not whether to repair, repeal, or replace the ACA.

Rather, it is how to redirect reform toward a goal the ACA does not explicitly pursue: ensuring that health care is delivered correctly all the time, as inexpensively as possible.

Recognizing that the process of forming a consensus will take several years to accomplish, I have also proposed two important actions to provide a stable foundation for a new and better health system: (1) taking immediate steps to hold health care spending at 17% of GDP and (2) shifting government's role from regulating via one-size-fits-all practice standards to requiring providers to have performance improvement programs with standard practices that ensure efficiency and effectiveness. Given dramatic differences in populations and resources across the country, providers should be rewarded for working accountably and transparently with purchasers, payers, and consumers to stop wasting 30 cents of every US dollar spent on health care.

Once we have built the world's most efficient and effective health system, our country will have available resources to pursue the ACA's goal of extending health care to all Americans— or whatever other goal is the consensus of the American people. (Even if a consensus cannot be reached, we will be better off for having halted waste.) The good news is that chaos is not permanent. Only a summary of the definition was presented at the beginning of the first chapter. Here it is, in full (italics mine):

> *chaos* [L, fr., Gk] 1) obs CHASM, GULF, ABYSS 2) a state of things in which chance is supreme 3) a state of utter confusion completely wanting in order: nature that is subject to no law or that is not necessarily uniform; *especially the confused unorganized state before the creation of distinctly organized forms*

We have the innovative talent to create distinctly organized, locally focused, world-class health care systems in the United States, but we must not let the chaos of our politics continue to get in the way. We must redirect reform to allow accountable, multistakeholder partnerships to build waste-free delivery systems, within the limits of 17% of GDP, using performance improvement programs that provide the best possible health care all the time, as inexpensively as possible. The money saved can then be used to improve the health of the entire population.

Notes

1. This case is made in a thought-provoking book I endorsed, Joe Flower's *Healthcare Beyond Reform* (Boca Raton, FL: CRC Press, 2012).
2. If you need inspiration for taking straightforward, decisive action like this, watch the classic Bob Newhart routine, "Stop It," at https://www.youtube.com/watch?v=Ow0lr63y4Mw.
3. Jeffrey C. Bauer. *Not What the Doctor Ordered*. New York: McGraw-Hill, 1998.
4. For an excellent example of public service in this area, see http://www.choosingwisely.org.

Chapter 7

Epilogue: Organizational Success Factors for Efficiency and Effectiveness

Introduction

Drawing on what Mark Hagland and I learned from researching dozens of case studies for the first edition of this book, we devoted the final chapter to a discussion of success factors common to providers that had mastered efficiency and effectiveness. Our list of common denominators was also based on our many years of consulting (Bauer) and journalistic (Hagland) interactions with organizations pursuing performance improvement and clinical excellence. We believe the list is still relevant, so I am including it in this revised edition as a checklist for leaders who are involved in redirecting reform for their organizations. Here are seven proven criteria to guide the overall process of responding to the new imperatives. Provider organizations may need to expand the list to encompass special dimensions of their particular mission and vision.

√ Standardization

Successful organizations are committed to standardizing data-driven production processes. Their leaders constantly seek to eliminate one of the major causes of poor quality and unnecessary cost in any industry: inappropriate and unexpected variability in production. A rich management literature shows how serious problems are created when employees dedicated to the same task are allowed to use different methods, tools, or supplies. The same literature also shows how management engineering determines the least-cost combination of resources that produces a product of defined quality—the outcome at the bottom of the U-shaped cost curves we all studied in Economics 101.

Production managers are taught how to push toward the bottom of the cost curve for a specified output because any other combination of inputs or processes is, by definition, wasteful. Getting there requires managers to set and enforce measurable standards for doing a job the right way with the right tools. Standard practices are not just for manufacturing. They are equally important in service industries where lives are on the line, as demonstrated by the phenomenal improvements that were made in commercial aviation when airline manufacturers started putting uniform instrumentation in cockpits and airlines started teaching all pilots to fly planes the same way based on scientific determination of best practices.

These principles were also applied to the administration of anesthetics, making modern anesthesia as safe as flying. Our case studies in the 2008 edition showed impressive gains that were obtained by applying the same principles to many other clinical services. The case for promoting standardization in health care is unambiguous. Of course, resistance to standardization is equally certain because physicians and nurses have been trained in so many different ways and have become accustomed to so many different products. Therefore, leaders must resist pleas to maintain the old way of doing things once the new standard is implemented. Multiple standards are inefficient at best and dangerous at worst. A standard should be flexible (see the next section on flexibility), but it should be *the* standard for performance within the organization.

The case studies in the first edition clearly demonstrated the need to put appropriate clinicians in charge of standardization—giving them authority, accountability, and resources to eliminate the waste that flows from undesirable variation in production. Standardization will not be easy, but it is absolutely essential for providers who plan to recover and reallocate wasted resources in a marketplace that has stopped paying more to subsidize their inefficiencies. Board members, ultimately accountable for the wise management of organizational resources, should put top priority on working with senior executives and clinical leaders to make standardization part of the corporate culture, as soon as possible if the task has not already been accomplished.

√ Flexibility

Efficiency and effectiveness are always moving targets in health care. The optimal way to produce any given medical service evolves constantly with the development of new drugs and devices, the publication of new research results, technological advances, and changes in the payment system. Consequently, standards need to be flexible over time. A standard that defines today's best combination of inputs for producing a service of predetermined quality is very unlikely to be a constant standard for years to come. Some standards will require only minor modification from time to time, while

others will need to be restructured dramatically and frequently. (As noted in previous discussion, inflexibility is one
of the biggest problems with regulatory practice standards.
Government agencies are almost never able to change practice standards as fast as changes in medical science and technology. In my experience, government standards are almost
always outdated by the time they are finalized.)

Consequently, managers and work groups responsible for
an organization's efficiency and effectiveness need to be given
permanent status and ongoing authority to change with the
times. Performance improvement cannot be organized as a
"one-shot" activity to be disbanded as soon as initial standards are promulgated. In all but the smallest organizations,
departments or divisions created to manage performance
improvement will need to become part of the permanent
organizational structure. Qualified consultants will be appropriate substitutes for internal resources in many situations,
especially for initiating the activities and teaching employees
how to manage performance improvement processes. If an
organization is unable to institutionalize performance improvement (a possible sign of serious structural problems that
must be addressed and resolved independent of performance
improvement), then long-term contracts for services from
qualified external experts should be pursued.

Whatever the best solution for a particular organization,
success depends on providing resources to support continual
revision of standards in accord with changes in medical science and technology. Active involvement in progressive
professional associations and periodic participation in
standards-focused meetings will also be important. Few provider organizations can reach the economies of scale to be
self-sufficient in keeping up with the changing criteria for efficiency and effectiveness. Fortunately, most organizations that
have the resources for do-it-yourself specification of standards
are also active in national organizations and conferences.
Leaders from organizations with more limited resources can

benefit immensely by interacting with their counterparts from exemplary institutions by belonging to national organizations and attending relevant meetings. It is a cost-effective way to stay flexible and respond to the imperatives.

√ Integration

The national leaders in cost and quality have highly integrated organizations, including their information technology (IT). Networked hardware and software are the norm because efficiency and effectiveness can only be built on a foundation of shared data and common IT platforms. Broadband connectivity, increasingly with wireless platforms, facilitates practitioners' access to patient data from all locations and timely interaction with interactive support systems. Information flows seamlessly between clinical care, operations, and finance. State-of-the-art network security regulates access, protects integrity, and ensures availability of the data when and where they are needed. Validity (i.e., meaningfulness) and reliability (i.e., accuracy) of all data are also assured by the professionals responsible for collecting, storing, and analyzing the numbers that drive production processes.

The national leaders in efficiency and effectiveness tend to be multi-institution organizations. Several providers have come together as a business enterprise to create economies of scale in infrastructure, including but not limited to their integrated IT systems. Although most of these provider organizations are single corporate entities created by mergers and acquisitions, formal affiliation agreements can also create business partnerships that achieve economies of scale. Outsourcing arrangements and provider-vendor partnerships have proven to be viable alternatives to mergers. Increasingly, these multi-institutional organizations include payers (e.g., health insurance companies) and even purchasers (e.g., employers)—

examples of the multistakeholder partnerships that I have actively promoted in previous chapters.

Two qualifications are important to discussion of integration. First, mergers to create multi-institutional systems of health care providers can go too far, creating diseconomies of scale and dysfunctional clashes in corporate culture. Astute leaders recognize the need to create systems that are big enough to afford necessary infrastructure—but not so big that they are unmanageable. Second, outsourcing does not necessarily mean that work will be done in another country. Significant economic advantages can often be gained by exporting some activities to "offshore" workers and computers located in other countries, but "off-site" outsourcing within the U.S. can also produce significant economic benefits.

√ Alignment

Alignment might seem like another word for integration, but the two concepts are different. I have personally observed several highly integrated delivery systems that are inefficient and ineffective because the stakeholders are not aligned. Alignment requires that everyone in the organization is pursuing the same short-term objectives and long-term goals. (I further assume that the shared goals are elimination of waste and reallocation of recovered resources to population health.) Organizations, large or small, are dysfunctional when internal stakeholders are pitted against each other in zero-sum games for personal income, budgets, space, personnel, power, and so on. Providers cannot reduce costs of consistent, appropriate, and safe top-quality health services if employees and business partners are competing. Aligned enterprises, on the other hand, have accomplished the difficult transition from win-lose to win-win within the organization.

The organizations in our previous case studies have done a remarkable job in eliminating wasteful competition between their stakeholders. They have created teams, for example, in which physicians, nurses, and pharmacists are "working for the good of the order" because all are rewarded for organizational success. Leaders must be sure that teamwork permeates the organizational culture. Most providers will discover room for improvement in this area and should be sure that their organization has appropriate resources, internal or external, for making necessary changes to establish teamwork as a core value.

Mark Hagland and I found that most or all physicians were employed by the health system in the successful cases we studied. This is important because physicians who are not employed tend to have private practices that compete with the health system. We also learned that the chief executives in most of our country's world-class organizations are also physicians. An employed medical staff and physicians in top leadership positions are becoming even more common among health systems recognized as the best in the country. It is a key characteristic of alignment in the new medical marketplace, as is an enterprise-wide commitment to meeting the ultimate goal of optimizing population health with an appropriate mix of inpatient, outpatient, and community-based services. Health systems that exist primarily to preserve a traditional hospital (i.e., acute care facility) will be lucky to survive competition from integrated multi-stakeholder organizations that are reinventing health care for the 21st century.

For health systems that do not formally align with purchasers and payers, leaders must be sure that the payment system does not become an impediment to doing the right thing. For example, disease management and prevention programs are valuable tools for lowering costs and eliminating waste, but they can be difficult to implement if third-party reimbursement still favors expensive inpatient services and episodic care. Leaders need to become actively involved in working with third-party health plans to align payment with cost and quality objectives. This point has been indirectly reinforced in recent reform efforts. Indeed, if there is one conclusion that would be accepted by all parties involved in the Affordable Care Act—proponents and opponents alike—it is that fee-for-service reimbursement that rewards volume must be replaced by payment mechanisms that reward value instead.

√ Leadership

The organizations surveyed for the original edition had, and still have, the great fortune of good, strong leadership. The officials responsible for strategic direction—board members, senior executives, medical and nursing staff officers, and caregiver champions—have a viable vision of the organization's potential, and they act accordingly. They know that standardizing performance is essential not only for efficiency and effectiveness but also for survival and growth.

A few organizations probably have enough resources, through endowments and royalties, to survive for a long time without responding to the marketplace imperatives. The fact that some of these well-off organizations are world leaders in efficiency and effectiveness demonstrates the true professionalism that should motivate all providers to improve, even if the marketplace were not demanding it. These well-positioned leaders are also looking beyond their own organizations to the future of health care in general and the needs of their own market areas in particular. They drive their organizations to respond to the expectations of purchasers, payers, and consumers. Community benefit is a major motivation, which facilitates appropriate collaboration with other stakeholders on all sides of the marketplace.

One attribute clearly stands out as a common descriptor of the successful organizations' leaders: sustained commitment. The leaders recognize that pursuit of efficiency and effectiveness is a long-term job. They are relentless in their pursuit of the least-cost combination of inputs to produce health services of predetermined quality. Consequently, the leaders are eager, willing, and able to move their organizations through the inevitable "rough patches" in early stages of work. Their commitment is sustained over time and across the enterprise, regardless of the roadblocks, because they know that performance improvement is the right and necessary thing to do for the health of the populations they serve.

√ Accountability

The remarkable accomplishments presented in the first edition's case studies were uniformly data driven, and the same holds equally true today. Leaders set achievable, quantifiable goals. They then collect and analyze meaningful, accurate numbers to gauge actual performance against stated, measurable objectives. Processes are continually refined until they yield cost reductions and the desired level of quality. Then, for reasons just presented in the discussion of flexibility, the process starts over because efficiency and effectiveness are moving targets in modern health care.

A quantitative definition of accountability may not be the first one to come to mind, but it is paramount when the goals are efficiency and effectiveness. An organization must have numbers to measure performance. In addition, stakeholders on the demand side of the marketplace are expecting more numbers for comparing the cost and quality of competing providers. Many customers are now selecting their providers by assessing the value of what they get for the money they spend on health care. This is the classic accountability of the law of the marketplace, as covered in Economics 101.

Accountability is often linked to transparency in contemporary discussions of health policy. Transparency is not essential to the economic concepts of efficiency and effectiveness, but it is becoming essential for success in the medical marketplace. A secretive (i.e., nontransparent) organization could be the least-cost producer of the top-quality good in a marketplace, but inaccessibility of its information will likely cause it to lose business to lesser, "open" organizations that publish their metrics for public review. Providers that are efficient and effective have nothing to hide and should publicize their accomplishments with great pride.

√ Creativity

The first edition's case studies and subsequent experience show that cost and quality leaders are impatient with the traditional ways of producing health care. They do not like the implications of business as usual. They embrace the challenge of doing something new, different, and better. After all, obedience to tradition explains a substantial portion of the problems in today's medical marketplace. America's leaders are eager not only to break the mold but also to shape new health care systems in a spirit of self-improvement and social responsibility.

Ironically, America's world-class health systems generally do not participate in reforms' demonstration projects. These creative organizations are constantly improving, while the demonstrations test a static model for several years. By the time a demonstration project has validated a different approach to health care, the organizations that originally created it are already doing something different and better. Innovative organizations and their business partners—not government demonstration projects—provide the inspiration for redirecting reform and prove that accountable American enterprise can build the world's best health care system, as evidenced by the world's healthiest population. Health reform needs to be redirected as quickly as possible toward this goal, one very unlikely to be reached by current proposals to repair, repeal or replace the Affordable Care Act. We need to find another way to have the best health care that can be produced with 17% of GDP. Why not get started now?

Index

About the Author

Dr. Jeffrey C. Bauer is an internationally recognized health futurist and medical economist. As an independent industry thought leader, he forecasts the evolution of health care and develops practical approaches to improving the medical sector of the American economy. He is widely known for his specific proposals to create an efficient and effective health care delivery system through multistakeholder partnerships and other initiatives focused in the private sector.

Dr. Bauer has published more than 250 articles, books, web pages, and videos on health care delivery over the past 45 years. He speaks frequently to national and international audiences about key trends in health care, medical science, technology, information systems, reimbursement, public policy, health reform, and creative problem solving. Dr. Bauer is quoted often in the national press and writes regularly for professional journals that cover the business of health care.

His latest book is *Upgrading Leadership's Crystal Ball: Five Reasons Why Forecasting Must Replace Predicting and How to Make the Strategic Change in Business and Public Policy* (Taylor & Francis, Boca Raton, FL, 2014). Other recent books include *Paradox and Imperatives in Health Care: How Efficiency, Effectiveness, and E-Transformation Can Conquer Waste and Optimize Quality* (with Mark Hagland; Productivity Press, New York, 2008) and *Statistical Analysis for Health Care Decision-Makers* (CRC Press, Boca Raton, FL, 2009). His two previous books are *Telemedicine and the Reinvention of Health Care: The*

Seventh Revolution in Medicine (with Marc Ringel; McGraw-Hill, New York, 1999) and *Not What the Doctor Ordered* (McGraw-Hill, New York, 1998).

As a consultant, he has assisted hundreds of provider, purchaser, and payer organizations with strategic planning and performance improvement. He served as industry thought leader for the Superior Consultant Company and (after acquisition) as vice president for health care forecasting and strategy for ACS, a Xerox Company, from 1999 to 2010. His previous consulting firm, The Bauer Group, specialized in consumer-focused strategic planning and development of clinical affiliation agreements for multihospital networks from 1984 to 1992.

In addition, Dr. Bauer has extensive academic experience. He was a full-time teacher and administrator at the University of Colorado Health Sciences Center in Denver from 1973 to 1984, where he held appointments as associate professor and as assistant chancellor for planning and program development. He also served concurrently for four years as health policy adviser to Colorado Governor Richard D. Lamm. From 1992 to 1998, Dr. Bauer was a visiting professor in administrative medicine at the Medical School of the University of Wisconsin–Madison, where he taught physician leaders how to evaluate research reports and other published studies. Prior to his career in health care, he worked on meteorology projects for the National Center for Atmospheric Research.

He received his PhD in economics from the University of Colorado–Boulder. He graduated from Colorado College in Colorado Springs with a B.A. in economics and completed a certificate in political studies at the University of Paris (France). During his academic career, he was a Boettcher Scholar, a Ford Foundation Independent Scholar, a Fulbright Scholar (Switzerland), and a Kellogg Foundation National Fellow. He is an elected member of the Association of Managers of Innovation and the Institute of Medicine of Chicago and is an honorary Fellow in the American Academy of Nurse Practitioners. Dr. Bauer lives in Chicago, where he occasionally displays his paintings in local art galleries. He is an avid fan of music and member of the Governing Board of the Chicago Symphony Association.